# Dreaming with
# GOD

### A Journey from Grief to the Divine

## ALEXANDRA DE AVALON

BALBOA
PRESS
A DIVISION OF HAY HOUSE

Copyright © 2014 Alexandra De Avalon.

All rights reserved. No part of this book may be used or reproduced by any means, graphic, electronic, or mechanical, including photocopying, recording, taping or by any information storage retrieval system without the written permission of the publisher except in the case of brief quotations embodied in critical articles and reviews.

Balboa Press books may be ordered through booksellers or by contacting:

Balboa Press
A Division of Hay House
1663 Liberty Drive
Bloomington, IN 47403
www.balboapress.com
1 (877) 407-4847

Because of the dynamic nature of the Internet, any web addresses or links contained in this book may have changed since publication and may no longer be valid. The views expressed in this work are solely those of the author and do not necessarily reflect the views of the publisher, and the publisher hereby disclaims any responsibility for them.

The author of this book does not dispense medical advice or prescribe the use of any technique as a form of treatment for physical, emotional, or medical problems without the advice of a physician, either directly or indirectly. The intent of the author is only to offer information of a general nature to help you in your quest for emotional and spiritual well-being. In the event you use any of the information in this book for yourself, which is your constitutional right, the author and the publisher assume no responsibility for your actions.

Any people depicted in stock imagery provided by Thinkstock are models, and such images are being used for illustrative purposes only.
Certain stock imagery © Thinkstock.

Printed in the United States of America.

ISBN: 978-1-4525-2157-2 (sc)
ISBN: 978-1-4525-2159-6 (hc)
ISBN: 978-1-4525-2158-9 (e)
Library of Congress Control Number: 2014915852

Balboa Press rev. date: 11/03/2014

For David's sister Amira, his cousins,
and all our children in heaven.

# Contents

Acknowledgments ............................................................... ix
Introduction ........................................................................ xi
Prologue  The Oak Tree Speaks ........................................ xv

| | | |
|---|---|---|
| Chapter 1 | Dreaming with God ........................................... | 1 |
| Chapter 2 | Friday, August 14 .............................................. | 5 |
| Chapter 3 | Gone Home ........................................................ | 9 |
| Chapter 4 | My Journey Begins ............................................ | 12 |
| Chapter 5 | Living in Two Worlds ....................................... | 14 |
| Chapter 6 | The Funeral ....................................................... | 17 |
| Chapter 7 | Visiting My Friends ........................................... | 22 |
| Chapter 8 | Miracles in El Salvador .................................... | 25 |
| Chapter 9 | The Doorway ..................................................... | 33 |
| Chapter 10 | The Tree of Knowledge and Spirituality ......... | 37 |
| Chapter 11 | The Cemetery .................................................... | 42 |
| Chapter 12 | Medicine Wheel ................................................. | 47 |
| Chapter 13 | Grieving ............................................................. | 52 |
| Chapter 14 | My Daughter, Amira, Arrives ........................... | 58 |
| Chapter 15 | Happy Birthday, David .................................... | 63 |
| Chapter 16 | The Healing World of Massage ........................ | 66 |
| Chapter 17 | David's Second Birthday in Heaven ................ | 71 |

| | | |
|---|---|---|
| Chapter 18 | A Matter of Time | 76 |
| Chapter 19 | Creating Avalon | 78 |
| Chapter 20 | Henry's Choice | 84 |
| Chapter 21 | Writing, a Christmas Gift | 87 |
| Chapter 22 | I Am Alive | 93 |
| Chapter 23 | Grief | 96 |
| Chapter 24 | The Final Transition | 99 |
| Chapter 25 | Healer, Heal Thyself | 105 |
| Chapter 26 | Connecting to the Other Side | 113 |

Conclusion The Oak Tree Speaks ..................................................121
About the Author..........................................................................123

# Acknowledgments

Thank you, God and the angels, for guiding me on this journey. You provided the miracles, the extraordinary events manifesting divine intervention in human affairs, which encouraged me to write this spiritual story.

Gracias Richard Abbot, husband and life partner, for engaging in our transformations, believing in me, and making my world a safer place to live.

Much gratitude to Peggy Umanzio and Carol Du Bey, my writing group, for support and inspiration on a weekly basis, which includes laughter and tears.

I'm eternally grateful to Debra Ratner for her valuable advice while she was editing my work and honoring me as a writer.

Appreciation to all those who gave love, encouragement, and insight.

# Introduction

*The most beautiful experience we can have is the mysterious.*
—Albert Einstein

In 1985 when I became pregnant, I was positive it would be a girl, the daughter I had always been dreaming about. I bought little pink outfits with lace and bonnets to match.

In April of 1986, the eighth month of my pregnancy, I had a dream about my grandmother, Trinidad, who had already passed on, and made her transition. I was floating in the night sky filled with stars. I saw a mansion made of stone with two huge wooden doors. I continued to fly over the doorway, and soon the doors opened wide. There was my grandmother, smiling as she welcomed me. I flew inside, and she continued to guide my way. She opened another door, and we entered a room full of baby cribs. I flew over the cribs, hoping to find my daughter.

I saw a crib that glowed, and the baby in it looked at me. Somehow I knew it was a boy. I flew down and picked him up in my arms. We smiled at each other. I heard his voice telling me, "Mom, I will be first. After me will come my sister." Then a brilliant fluttering light came soaring from a distance and stayed beside me. A young girls voice from the light said, "Mom, wait for me. I will be with you as soon as I can." I held the baby boy in my arms, and I could see my grandmother standing near a tall window, as if she was expecting a storm to arrive. The curtains started to blow.

When I woke up, I still did not want to believe I was having a baby boy first. So when David was born, he wore a pink baby outfit home.

This book is written nineteen years after David's transition. Emotional pain became my teacher in my search for healing. Constant miracles inspired me to write about my spiritual journey with grief. Healing my physical and emotional body has been continuous. I wish to share my insights, understanding, and hope.

My experience with God confirms that I am not alone in anything that happens to me. Angels and beings of light continue to give me comfort and awareness of all the miracles that come my way.

There isn't a day, not a moment that I do not miss my son, David. It will always be like this. What I can do is redirect my energy and honor his existence as he lives in God's mansion.

David at four years old.

## Ode on Intimations of Immortality

But there is a tree, of many, one,
A Single field which I have look'd upon,
Both of them speak of something that is gone:
The pansy at my feet
Doth the same tale repeat:
Whither is fled the visionary gleam?
Where is it now, the glory and the Dream?

—William Wordsworth

# Prologue
## The Oak Tree Speaks

The day breathes heat. As usual I face the highway, towering over all movement below. A car suddenly swerves directly toward me. The ferocious impact shakes me down to my roots. Metal, crumpling up like foil, traps a child in the car, a boy, his small limp body unable to move. My branches are unable to pull him out. If only I could hold this child, his pain would leave. I weep as I see a beautiful light leap out and flutter around me. I weep for what is to come.

The moments gather, bringing two women draped in shadows. They come holding a white sword, an abalone shell, and a feather. The taller of the two, with raven hair, presses her body against mine, whispering words that stir memories of long ago. Her heart beats with the rhythm of excruciating pain. We understand each other. She knows the old ways. This is why she is here. With the shell in one hand and the feather in the other, she fans the old familiar smoke of sage around me.

The sage begins to lift some of the sadness the boy has left behind. The other woman takes the white sword and pushes it into the earth below me. Mother Earth gasps, releasing her memory.

The two women, like pillars ready to crumble, reach for each other. Their arms entwined, they slowly slip away.

I witness the day in its final light. I gaze down at the sword, which has become the shadow of a golden cross glowing beneath me.

## *Ode on Intimations of Immortality-continued*

Our birth is but a sleep, and forgetting:
The Soul that rises with us, our life's Star,
Hath had elsewhere its setting and cometh from afar:
Not in entire forgetfulness,

And not in utter nakedness,
But trailing clouds of glory do we come
from God, who is our home;
Heaven lies about us in our infancy!
Shades of prison-house begin to close
Upon the growing Boy,
But he beholds the light, and whence it flows,
He sees it in his joy

—William Wordsworth

# CHAPTER 1

## Dreaming with God

*The only thing we take with us is love.*
—David (communication received in a meditation)

### David August 1992

My name is David. Please say it like a Spanish person—Dahveed. I have been dreaming with God. Right now I am six and a half years old, and I have always wanted to be a doctor.

My mom is sad a lot these days, but when I touch her beautiful black hair, it makes her smile. Mom is expecting a baby, and as big brother, it is up to me to let that unborn baby know who our family is. When Mom is resting, I tiptoe into her bedroom and whisper to my mommy's tummy what our family is about. Then I give mommy a kiss so she will remember me.

In the morning the sound of Mom's voice wakes me up. I have pictures in my head of angels who tell me stories about being good and bad. We all have angels. There are special angels who take care of people who have done bad things. They help these people talk to God. All the angels tell me how heaven works. At home and in school I draw these pictures because it helps me tell their stories better. When I show my pictures to Mom, she listens and tries to understand everything I say. She asks me lots of questions about what the angels do in heaven.

Today we visit my grandmother, my mother's mom. I call her Nana. Next to my mom, she is my favorite person in the world. Nana likes to have parties all the time. I always like the parties because my cousins come over and we all play in the pool. I am their Spanish spy, bringing them pieces of grown-up conversations that I translate into English.

I have an uncle who is the tallest man I know. On this day he smiles at me and says, "Hi, David."

Looking up into his eyes, I say, "I am going to be with God soon."

The smile leaves his face, and he says, "David, don't say that. That would make everyone very sad."

"I don't understand," I say. "Why is it sad to be with God?"

My uncle does not answer, but his face becomes worried. It is time to go look for my cousins, and I take off in a run.

The angels had told me that the time to leave my family was getting close.

***Spirit asks:*** *Have you experienced angels or a loved one who has passed on giving a message to you?*

David beside Nana's pool. He is waiting for his cousins to arrive.

David's picture of four good angels with wings, each holding a cross. God is seated in the middle. To the left of God is the person who has done bad things. Above God in a red bubble are angels with a person who had done bad things.

# CHAPTER 2

## Friday, August 14

*Catch the kiss that is given to you and give it back, never wipe it away. You never know if it will be the last time.*
—David (communication received in a meditation)

## David

Today, Friday, August 14, 1992, is my last day here. An angel woke me up to tell me I will be going home to God. It begins—the sadness in my heart about how I will miss my mom and family. Friends in school, I know I will miss them too. The angel told me he will be with me all day. He said God has a special plan for me. When I get to heaven, God will tell me how I am going to help him.

There's a knock on my bedroom door. "David, wake up. Time to get dressed," my mom says,

"'Kay, mom."

I jump out of bed, and I think I will wear my favorite clothes today. Found it, -my hot pink T-shirt and black shorts with guitars all over them. Next I find white socks with pink stripes and black sneakers 'cause it all has to match. Finally I put on my black cap, grab my gray bag, and stuff it with my favorite toys. I'm ready.

Ran to the bathroom and I hear my mom yell, "David, brush your teeth. Your cereal is ready." She forgets that I like brushing my teeth 'cause my grandma says I have beautiful teeth and she likes to see them when I smile.

It's time to get in the car. My mom is going to Mount Diablo Hospital 'cause her baby is not growing right, so they have to take it out. I'm supposed to go to school, but I want to go to the hospital with her first. The angel tells me it is important that I go.

Pouring lots of kisses on my mom, I say, "Please, please let me come with you. I want to make sure you're okay. Please, please, Mommy, please."

She waits and answers, "Yes, your stepdad will take you to school afterward."

We drive to the Hospital. When we get there, Mom is taken to a room where they put wires on her. She tells me everything is going to be okay. As I wrap my arms around her, she kisses the top of my head. "Mom, I love you always."

She takes hold of my face in her hands and says, "I love you too, angel face," and she kisses me on my forehead. As I let her go, the nurse takes me away from the room. Through a round glass window we can see each other. Mom blows me a kiss and then throws it to me. Like a baseball, I catch it and place it on my cheek. It's my turn. I blow her a kiss and then throw it. She catches it and puts it on her cheek. This will be the last time she will see me. We smile as they take her away into another room. My heart is sad again. I feel the strong love I have for her. It will be with me forever.

My stepdad tries to comfort me. He drives me to school. When we arrive, my feet drag. I don't want to go inside. "Please, please let me go back to the hospital with you. I want to be with my mom."

I repeat this, in my pouting and begging voice, and he finally changes his mind. We get back in the car, and I sit in the front seat with my toy bag. After I open my bag, I start to play with some the toys and think of my best friends in school, who I will miss.

As we drive on the freeway, my stepdad's eyes start to close. He looks like he is sleeping. I look up and suddenly see a tree. My body smashes hard into the shattering metal surrounding me. A light so bright holds me. My angel tells me not to be afraid. I feel myself moving all around, free. Surprised, I see myself in the air. The angel puts his wings around me, and we fly. There is no pain, only light, only God.

**Spirit asks: *Do you believe that death is a return to Heaven?***

David giving a kiss to his mother, Alexandra, on his fourth birthday

# CHAPTER 3

## Gone Home

*When we are born the waves of energy carry us into the light. When we leave our body, it is the same. There is no difference.*
—Spirit, Divine Presence

### Alexandra August 14th

I woke up in a dream that will last forever. Strong intuition spoke. Something was wrong. I was still feeling groggy, realizing that I really had lost the baby I was carrying. My mind was cloudy. Nurses spoke in hushed voices with long, lingering stares. I started asking questions, and all I heard was, "I don't know." They said my husband would not be able to pick me up because he had been in an automobile accident. He was at John Muir Hospital. That was all they knew. An administrator from John Muir had called my sister Denise to take me there. We were to go through the emergency entrance. A nurse assigned to us would be waiting for us.

As we drove to John Muir Hospital, Denise and I tried to figure out what could have happened.

We pulled up in front of the emergency entrance. I was still feeling wobbly, so my sister held my arm as we walked in. We went up to a guard sitting behind a podium and told him who we were. He called someone, and in seconds a doctor came through two flapping doors. The anguish in the doctor's face made me realize, without hearing, that David had been in the car. My soul screamed. This sound, buried deep inside of me, broke free.

It was the wailing sound of a mother whose child has been ripped from her. My body collapsed, but not the sound. The sound is ancient. It has memory. It is timeless.

I was quickly surrounded by people on staff who carried me into a special room. Cloudiness and a few soft voices stayed with me. The doctor explained to me that they had tried to revive David three times. The doctor asked if I wanted to see David. My mind raced, and when I looked at my sister, I asked her to be my eyes and to remember it all in detail. I wanted to remember David as I last saw him. When I was ready, I would ask her to tell me what now she was going to see. Everyone left the room and I was alone, sitting in a chair.

Suddenly I felt something enter. My eyes quickly scanned the room, hoping to find what I was feeling. I heard rushing moving sounds all around me. I stood up and said, "David, are you here?"

A strong wave of energy rushed through me, wanting to hold me but not able to. It flew around me fast and swirled, and then it went through me again. I was crying with relief that David was still with me. I reached out to hold him. I closed my eyes, and I could feel him.

"David," I said, "I love you, *Papito*. You know you cannot stay with me. You have to go to God soon." He didn't budge. Using my mommy voice to guide my son, I said, "David, I am going to call my grandma and Jesus to take you home. You need to go into the light with them. They will take you to God." Shaking, I started to pray, "Dear Jesus and Mama Trini, please take care of my David. I trust that he will be safe with you. Please show him your light so he can see you and know where to go." The rushing movement of energy began again.

"David, listen to your mom," I said, unable to control my tears. "You need to go *now*." The last rush of energy went through me like a huge wave taking parts of me, and leaving only silence.

Lost in that moment was another voice, the baby I had never heard or held in my arms. Only my body remembers and grieves the memory. Years later while I was attending a natural birth, I observed that birth contractions were waves of life energy. This energy was the same as I had experienced with David on the day he went home.

**Spirit asks: Have you experienced people, or yourself, as waves of energy?**

# CHAPTER 4

## My Journey Begins

*Forgive everything, yes, everything.*
—David

### David August 14th

It takes time to get to heaven. Pictures of my family are in me. When I see my mom, I am there with her. I want to hold her, but I can't, so I run into her as always. She can feel me. It makes me so happy. Then I see Nana sitting on her bed and crying. She does not notice I am there. The pictures are moving faster. I see that my cousins, my Mami Chita, my *tias* (aunts), uncles, and everyone is so sad. No one told me it would be like this, not even my guardian angel.

My mom has asked me to go with Jesus and Mama Trini. I do what my mom asks. I see a great light and faces I recognize. Clouds, clouds, clouds all around me. A gathering of light carrying me into the heart of God. Colors quickly change me as I burst and blend into everything. Time has released me. I am one with God. God fills me, and I begin to understand why I am here.

I start to see pictures of children dying in a place called Somalia. They look scared and lost. I feel a deep need to help them get back home. Then I think of my family, and I want to help them too. I want to let them know that I was still alive.

I begin to see more pictures of my family and how much they are crying. I see my mom lying in bed alone, and it makes me very sad inside. Then the pictures switch to the lost children. I can feel how scared and sad they are because they want to see their mothers and fathers. I am able to be in two places at the same time, and it is okay. The more I help the children and my family, the bigger the love I feel for everything. I see that love is in everyone, and that is what we take to heaven.

As I watch everyone, I begin to feel and see the importance of forgiving. I can see when the light is not as strong in people and that not all the children want to come with me. Some want to stay with their families or where they feel loved. I see some of my family really upset and angry at what happened to me. It seems that the more we love, the stronger our light becomes. Forgiving makes us free to love, and heaven is love.

**Spirit asks: Is the focus of all our experience to find our way back to love?**

# CHAPTER 5

## Living in Two Worlds

*You own nothing.*
—David

### Alexandra August 15th

I was drowning in my mother's bed. Her aroma no longer calmed me. My eyes remained shut like a vault. My body started to stir, recognizing that something was in the room. My heart began fluttering, I knew that David was here. As I opened my eyes, they welcomed a glowing emerald green light sparkling in front of me.

"David," I said in a deep sad voice, "why are you here? I told you to go home. You are supposed to be with God." In a very eager voice, David said, "Mom, God has given me permission to come back and help you and the family. I have so much to tell you. Please listen."

David shared what happened in heaven and what he and God talked about. When he finished sharing everything, I understood several important things.

First, David had changed. He sounded more mature and very wise. His experience with God had transformed him. Second, David was my proof that we are eternal, that death is only a transformation from the physical to the spiritual. David's soul went back home and continues to live his life. He is in a sacred place, sharing his experience through telepathic communication and at times visiting me.

This was the beginning of many miracles. What he is experiencing with God is something I can never, ever give him. He is safe. I learned the pain of loss and grief as a mother. At times it was almost unbearable to be alive. David's spiritual gifts continue to give me comfort and acceptance. He has become my teacher.

That day I heard a knock on the door and did not want to get up. David said, "I will be with you for a while. I will let you know when I have to leave. I am here to help you now, Mom." My heart cried as tears ran down my face because I knew it was true. All that he had said was true. I got up to open the door.

God also knocked on a door, the doorway of life and death. It became a door that I could never close. Sometimes I wished that I could walk through this doorway and be with David.

**Spirit asks: *Do you believe there is a purpose for Pain?***

## *Ode on Intimations of Immortality-continued*

Behold the Child among his new born blisses,
A six year's darling of a pigmy size!
See, Where 'mid work of his own hand he lies,
Fretted by sallies of his mother's kisses,
With light upon him from his father's eyes!
See, at his feet some little plan or chart,
Some fragment from his dream of human life,
Shaped by himself and newly-learned Art;
A wedding or a festival,
A mourning or a funeral;
and this hath now his heart.

—William Wordsworth

# CHAPTER 6

## *The Funeral*

> There is a Cosmic Law that connects us to our
> destiny of birth and transition of which we
> do not completely understand. We are a mystery.
> —Spirit (communication received in a meditation)

### Alexandra August 21<sup>st</sup>

It is the day of the funeral. I have been talking to David since early in the morning. He wanted me to let everyone know that he was still alive, that his life had not been wasted, that he was fulfilling his destiny, and especially that God does exist.

He asked me to speak at the funeral in both Spanish and English. He said it would help everyone heal and release some of their sadness.

I have decided to wear a white dress to connect me with the place of light where David is. Wearing black is to acknowledge that the soul is traveling through a place of shadows, but David is light, my light. Yesterday I had a very significant inspiration. Give him your favorite crystal, the one from Madagascar. It must be buried with him. Only my sisters knew that I was going to place this quartz crystal in his hand. It became our special secret. When the family gathered the day before the burial, I placed the crystal in David's right hand.

All has been arranged for the funeral, the burial, and the wake to follow at my mother's home. Today is another hot, sticky day. It feels very surreal as I address everyone at the funeral home. My brother Eddy had arranged that throughout the service they play music from the movie sound track of "Somewhere in Time," with Christopher Reeves, one of my favorite films. At the end of the service Eddy gives me the tape. I realize that I will never be able to play it because the memories will be extremely emotional for me.

As I approach David's coffin, I see him dressed in his favorite red cap and Batman T-shirt. I kiss the freckle below his right eye. The crystal is still there under his right hand. I whisper in his ear, "It is only a matter of time."

As I stand in front of the podium, I see my family, friends, coworkers, and people I have not seen in years, and I feel the blessing of their love. Remembering David's words that this was a time of healing, I gather my thoughts and speak from my heart. When I speak, David is also speaking. My grandfather had been a psychic/medium back in El Salvador. His legacy feels very strong in me as I am channeling David. I believe God has been preparing me for this role.

Speaking in Spanish and in English, David's message is delivered. "We are here for such a short time. It is important that you remember we are eternal. Love is what brings us here, and love is what takes us home. It was my time to go to God and help him. God has asked me to help guide the children of Somalia that have lost their way to heaven. When they see me, they are not afraid, so they follow me home. I am growing up here in heaven. The love that we have here never stops. I am a part of you, and you are a part of me always."

Lots of other words flow through me, never to be captured again. The effect of the message fills everyone with tears and love that can only be healing.

Oakmont Cemetery in Lafayette, California, is on top of a hill surrounded by trees. On this day many groups of people seek shade from the beautiful branches that hover near the grave site. David is buried in the garden of peace.

Arriving at my mother's house, I see a familiar face that pours love into me. It is Ricardo, my ex-husband, whom I had married at the age of nineteen. The last time I saw him was about ten years ago. Ricardo was not David's father; our marriage had only lasted seven years. We embrace when we see each other. He gently holds me in his arms and whispers, "We need to find a special time to talk. I have something very important to tell you."

What I find myself doing is comforting all the people around me. My tears are soft, filled with grace and understanding. This is how I connect with those who have come to honor the passing of my child.

Phyllis, one of my oldest friends from my place of work, beckons me to sit next to her. She has a small box in her hand. As I sit down next to her, she hands me the box wrapped in purple paper with a beautiful silky purple ribbon. I am very touched by this moment. Many years ago Phyllis had lost twins, and she was one of the few people where explanations and comforting words were not necessary. I open the box, and there is a little card that says, "Somewhere in Time, Love Phyllis." My hands start to shake as I unwrap the purple tissue paper that holds a violet crystal ball. As I hold it up to the light, I see lots of tiny bubbles inside of it. Written on a little gold sticker are the words "Somewhere in Time," the name of the crystal ball. There is immense love at this moment.

We look into each other's eyes and hold each other's spirits. It is as if we had become friends to create this moment. God has given me another miracle.

Across the room I see Ricardo, who waves at me. I tell Phyllis that Ricardo wants to talk to me, and I give her a kiss on the cheek. I walk over to where Ricardo is waiting, take his hand, and say, "Let's talk."

We go to the rose garden in the backyard and sit down. Looking at the swimming pool, I think of the last time I saw David jumping in the pool, laughing, so filled with life. Ricardo's kind eyes bring me back to my reality. "Alexandra," he says, "David came to visit me last night in a dream."

I am suddenly filled with emotions I have no name for. "He was surrounded in a white golden light. He asked me to tell you that you are the best mom he ever had and that he is always with you and to thank you for the crystal you gave him. He knows it is your favorite crystal, and its light will always connect you to him. He then showed it to me. It is a long clear quartz crystal that he holds in his right hand."

I gasp, riveting sobs flowing out of me. He holds me until I finally stop crying.

I look into his eyes and say, "Yes, I put the crystal in his right hand as I kissed his beautiful little body good-bye. I told him the light will always connect us because God is light. I put the crystal in his right hand because it sends or releases energy out and the left hand receives energy." I thank Ricardo for being a messenger and giving me another miracle. Ricardo is a gifted psychic like my grandfather. That is one of the reasons why I married him.

David especially chose Ricardo to give me his message because they had never met and Ricardo did not know of our secret. David proved to me again that he was communicating from the other side. He wanted to make sure I knew I was not making any of this up. Phyllis's gift was a message as well, reminding me of what I had whispered to David—that it is only a matter of time.

*Spirit asks: Have you experienced Connection with someone on the other side? Do you believe there is no separation?*

# CHAPTER 7

## Visiting My Friends

*The essence of who I am is released to
empower the essence of who you are.*
—David (communication received in a meditation)

### David, September 1992

I miss my friends. God said I can visit anyone through special dreams. God told me that these dreams create a place where we can talk to people we love. It is love that helps us see each other. So I did.

I dreamt with five of my closest friends. They were happy to see me because they had been so sad. I told them where I was and what I was doing for God. They asked me lots of questions. It became important to prove to them that our dreams together were real. So in their dreams I told and showed them what toy they would be getting from me. We were happy and sad at the same time. We did not want to say good-bye, but finally it was time. Before I left, I asked them for a favor. It was something I needed to do for my mom. They promised they would help.

First it was time to take care of my friends, and I needed my mom's help. She would help prove to my friends that I was real.

When I got to my mom's bedroom, she was asleep. I waited for her to wake up. I saw her move, so I knew she felt me near her. My mom can always see my body of light. Her sad eyes opened, and in a soft voice she asked, "David, angel face, why are you here, my love?"

"Mom, you have to go visit my friends at my day care. I told them you would."

"What do you mean, David? " she asked.

I explained to my mom what was happening, and she said she would help. She told me that first she needed to call and get permission from the day care office for her visit. It needed to be okayed with my friends' parents. She would let me know what they said.

"Mom," I said, "please hurry up. I don't want my friends to forget. Let me show you what toys I want you to bring."

We went to my room. It is very hard for her to part with anything of mine, but she had to keep my promise.

# Alexandra

David gave me the task to call the day care facility and ask how David's classmates were doing. The director shared how emotional it was the day they announced David's death. Some children had to be sent home. Three weeks have passed, and his closest friends are still grieving deeply. I asked her if I could speak to the children and explain what happened and maybe share something of David's toys. She said she would need to get their parents' permission and would call me in a few days.

It was arranged. Only five parents gave permission.

I arrived with a box of toys in my arms. It was like carrying my child. David's teacher was waiting for me. She took me to a reading room where I sat in a little chair. They brought the five children in. Inside of me I heard David say, "See, Mom, I told you they would come."

I held back the tears, and in a quivering voice I welcomed them. They sat down on the floor and crossed their legs. They looked at me with so much tenderness, and finally one of them asked. "Can you tell us how the accident happened?" I briefly told them and ended it by saying David was with God.

Jennie, one of David's closest friends, said, "Yes, we know. David told us."

Then Mark said, "David said you would be giving us some of his toys. He said I could have his car."

My heart raced. I kept telling myself, "It's true. It is all true. It is real, and I am not making any of this up."

I pulled the box toward me, and I said, "Okay, come get your toys."

The children were filled with excitement. We shared laughter and smiles. It was remarkable how they understood what was happening. Then they sat down again. Looking up at me, Jennie said, "David asked us to do something for you."

They all stood up and formed a line. Jennie came first. She put her arms around me and said, "David wanted you to hug us as if you were hugging him. He wants to thank you for loving him so much."

They all came and hugged me one by one. I could feel my David through the arms of these very beautiful and special children. It was a way to say good-bye, the last physical embrace of my child, whom I could never hold again.

As I was getting ready to leave, the children and some of the teachers took me to the schoolyard where they had planted a tree in memory of David. The tree is still there, watching the children play, laugh, and grow.

***Spirit asks:*** *Do you have a way of communicating with the spirit world?*

# CHAPTER 8

## Miracles in El Salvador

*I am participating in the creation of life. I am also with you in awareness. Not too much has changed.*
—David (communication received in a meditation)

### Alexandra, October 1992

Two months have passed since David's transition. The month of October with its autumn colors reminds me that the earth is also preparing to experience the loss of life. Halloween was David's favorite holiday. I remember making him a silly Batman cape. He loved it and wore it for months. What will I do this Halloween? I am afraid of all the things that will not happen.

I had a dream with David last night. We were in this old house with lots of rooms. I saw David walk in. I was filled with so much happiness. I tried scooping him up in my arms, but I couldn't. "David, come with me." He looked sad and did not speak.

"Hold out your hand," I said. He did, and I was able to hold it. "David, pray with me. I can bring you back." I felt his warm hand, his body moving through waves of energy. It was working. I started praying out loud. Then my prayers, interwoven with sobs, woke me up. I was alone again.

Another time I heard and felt David urgently trying to connect with me. I had laid down for a nap since it was impossible to sleep at night. "Mom, Mom, it's me. Wake up. I need to talk to you." I opened my eyes and saw his flickering green light. I smiled and said, "Yes, my love, what do you want?'

"Mom," he said, "God wants us to go to El Salvador. We need to find the place where the children with no families live. We both need to go and help them. This is really important, Mom. God said you will know what to do. How are we going to do this?"

"David, I am not sure what you are asking me. I have not been to El Salvador in years. I wouldn't know where to begin to search for this place."

"Mom, God said he would help us. We just need to go and help these kids."

"David, let me think about it, and I will let you know how we can work this out."

Somehow I knew we had to do this. I called a few of my close friends, and shared David's request. They got really excited and a plan began to unfold. My dear friend Phyllis gave a check for two hundred dollars. I was amazed. Two other girlfriends from work said they would help me collect more money and toys. By the end of the week I had four thousand dollars, a big suitcase full of clothes, and a huge old army duffel bag filled with toys and stuffed animals.

It seemed that God did have a plan and we were just following orders.

I called my favorite aunt in El Salvador, Tia Rosita. We had always remained in communication throughout the years. She had written me a very loving letter expressing her sadness over David's passing. She had met him when he was about two years old. Now it was great to hear her voice. I told her about my quest, and she agreed to help. She asked me to come stay with her and said she would gather family and friends to help find the orphanage.

I arrived in El Salvador on October 31, the Day of the Dead, All Hallows' Eve. In Ancient times it was said to be the day when the veil that separates earth from heaven is the thinnest. The Scots called it *Sowans,* the Day of Death and Renewal. Halloween will never be the same for me for so many reasons. Unexpectedly I was happy and excited about this journey. I was on an adventure with David.

Tia Rosita let me relax for a day. I told her all about my experiences with David. She understood and believed me. She reminded me that my great-grandmother was a *curandera,* a healer or medicine woman. She said I was born with the gift of my ancestors and that returning to El Salvador was a sign to remember this.

The next morning my aunt let me know that she had invited certain family members and friends for lunch so that they could help me. I was eager to find out how all of this was going to work. By noon everyone started to arrive. To my surprise it was my cousin Nenita and her father, my *tio,* Victor Elynor, who had information for me.

When they heard why I was coming, they were thrilled because they knew of an orphanage that was in desperate need. The building was falling apart. At one time Catholic nuns ran it, but they had had to abandon their project because of a lack of funds. The community of San Miguel had come together and asked my uncle for help, because he was the president of the local Lions Club, well known as a charitable organization.

My uncle and cousin saw me as an answer to their prayers. Quickly we got down to basics. We made plans to go visit the orphanage of San Miguel. I could feel David's happiness. His presence was with me everywhere I went.

Soon we arrived in San Miguel. The person in charge for that day gave us a tour of the orphanage. As we walked around, we talked about what was needed. The orphanage at one time had been a *hacienda*. A hacienda is circular. It has corridors all around, leading to all the rooms, with a patio garden in the middle. What I saw were walls in disrepair. The kitchen stove had broken down, so they were using a pit of broken bricks filled with wood where flames managed to cook whatever was placed on them. The bedrooms where the girls slept had a variety of twelve worn-out twin-size beds where thirty girls made room for each other. Nails above the beds held what they owned. Noticing all the candles, I soon realized there were no light fixtures in the rooms. The boy's dormitory was in the old gymnasium behind the hacienda, where cots were filled with hay. There were only ten cots and twenty-five boys.

The nuns had created classrooms where local teachers now took turns donating their time to teach. They held special training classes in sewing for the older girls and landscaping for the older boys, hoping to provide a trade. As soon as the children turned sixteen, they had to leave to make room for the younger ones to be taken in. I was told they usually left to live on the streets. They had no family or home to go to.

We all agreed that getting beds with mattresses was a priority. Providing bed clothing and fixing the stove would be next. Then we would have to fix the roof before the rains came in January.

There was so much to do, and I had enough money to do all of it. The American dollar goes a long way in Central America.

In the next couple of weeks, everything was arranged. Before I returned to the States, I went back for my last visit. They had prepared a farewell celebration. The smaller children sang songs for me. I was given lovely pictures with words of gratitude from the older children.

Then the miracle happened. As we were walking to the boy's

dorm, they all came out. They were laughing and smiling. One of them took my hand, and then they all started singing a song David and I used to sing, *"Cielito Lindo"* (Lovely Little Heaven). As I looked into their beautiful faces, it was as if I saw David's eyes in many of them. They were the brown round eyes of my son looking back at me, singing to me, loving me, holding me.

***Spirit asks:*** *Are you called to do things that are beyond your power? What do you do then?*

Orphanage in San Miguel, El Salvador. The broken-down kitchen that needed repair.

Children sleeping on the floor at the orphanage.

## Ode on Intimations of Immortality-continued

Those shadowy recollections,
which, be they what they may,
Are yet the fountain-light of all our day,
Are yet a master-light of all our seeing,

—William Wordsworth

# CHAPTER 9

## The Doorway

### Alexandra, The Past

It all began with my great-grandmother, Silveria, who lived in the world of spirits. She was a curandera, or medicine woman of Mayan decent. She was the healer of her village, using herbs, cures, chants, spirits, and hands-on healing, removing bad spirits and deciphering dreams. This ancient Mayan medicine worked. Her son, my grandfather, was blessed with this gift, as am I.

My grandfather's name was Papa Chepe. Others knew him as Don Jose Maria Zepeda. He was psychic and a medium. Papa Chepe would go into a trance and commune with the family spirits of those in the room. He would give advice on how to help those who needed healing. He recommended herbs and other methods that would help their ailments, even emotional ones. Sometimes people would want to know about their future, and he would tell them. These séances were held in his home in a small town called Armenia in the country of El Salvador.

My grandfather had one big problem—my grandmother. Dona Trinidad Quesada de Zepeda did not want these activities in her home. It annoyed her to have people coming in and out in the evenings. She was a staunch Catholic who prayed that he would stop all of these activities. Her prayers were never answered.

The séances were held in the evening around the dining room table. Papa Chepe would start by inviting spirits in. Then as they came, he would tell the people in attendance which spirits had arrived. Sometimes a person would ask to speak to someone specifically, like a departed wife. He would go into a trance and commune with the spirits around him, passing on messages that brought hope and acceptance. Papa Chepe did this for many years. When my mother was sixteen, he passed away. He died of cancer because he'd had a very bad habit of chewing tobacco.

At the age of four, I started to see spirits. I remember running into my grandmother Trinidad's bedroom, jumping on her bed, and with an animated voice, sharing what I had seen. Because it was me, her beloved grandchild, she held me tenderly in her arms and asked me what they looked like. Then she would say that I had seen my great-grandmother or her cousin who just passed away, and she would ask me, "What did they have to say?" She did this in the most natural way, and my gift of seeing those who had passed on never bothered her. Maybe they reminded her of her husband, my grandfather, and it was a way to stay connected with him.

My grandmother nurtured my spirit for the future. It was okay for me to talk to those who had left their bodies and were transitioning to the other side. I was a medium, and my grandmother knew it. I was being given valuable training for the healing work that I would be called to do. She encouraged me, without knowing that it would be my greatest ability in connecting with her great-grandson, far in the future. Communicating with David is as natural as my experiences were then.

My mother was the pioneer of our family. She moved to the United States, and a year later brought us there. My grandmother held my brother and me closely to her as we all arrived in San Francisco, on the first of the year, 1958. Years later I was told how my grandmother had sold all her property to help pay for us to be here.

My gift of communicating with the spirit world got stronger because I was never afraid. I knew they needed to tell me something important. Sometimes it was to say how they died, or they had a message for a loved one. As a teenager I became more sensitive and in tune with the world of spirits. I could hold objects in my hand and see images of people and places or hear conversations.

One afternoon I was in my bedroom, looking at a special treasure box of things people had given me. My grandmother, who had remarried several years earlier, had given me eyeglasses that had belonged to my step-grandfather, Papa Roberto, who had recently passed away.

I was sitting on a small chair with my arms resting on my desk, holding his eyeglasses, remembering his happy round face and kind eyes. I started to cry, missing him and remembering how generous he had been in spending time with me and all the children of our family. Suddenly I felt a presence. I had a twin-size bed, and in the middle I could see weight pressing down on the bed as if somebody had just sat there. I knew it was Papa Roberto, even though I could not see him.

I called out to him, "You are visiting me. What do you need, Papa?"

I could not hear his voice, but I felt this energy that was warm. I realized he was upset that I was crying. So I asked him, "You don't want me to cry, do you?"

Then I heard an inner voice, his voice in Spanish saying, *"No llores mas por mi, tu y tu abuela. No lloren mas por mi."* ("No more crying for me, you, and your grandma. No more crying for me.")

I promised him that I would tell my grandmother and we would stop crying. I saw the weight on the bed lift, and I took the eyeglasses and put them back in my box. Then I said, "I promise, Papa, next time I see your eyeglasses, I will not cry." I put the box away in my closet, and I got up to tell my grandmother. As I was leaving my bedroom, I knew he was still there. Slowly turning, I said to him, "I love you, Papa."

It was then that I could feel him leave. I knew my grandmother had been very sad because I could hear her crying at night. Papa Roberto also knew this. He needed to remind her that he was still alive and taking care of us in a different way now. Slowly I walked into the kitchen where my grandmother was cooking. She looked up at me and immediately said, *"Que pasa* (what is it)?"

In a soft voice I said, "Papa Roberto just visited me, Grandma."

She said, "Come sit down. Tell me what he said." I told her everything that happened and especially my promise to him. She said, "Okay, we will light candles for him, and we will not cry. We must tell your mother when she comes home so we can all pray together. Our crying is reaching him and worrying him. We cannot worry him anymore."

As I reflect upon that time, I realize that all the women in our family must have been grieving for him. Papa Roberto was the only man around our family. My own father was in and out of our lives. He embodied the typical Latin male, a bee mesmerized by all the flowers around him. We were missing a strong male presence, the father who protected, mentored, and financially supported his own, and kept the family calm in a crisis. We had all become very strong women, highly opinionated from living in survival mode.

**Spirit asks:** *Can you feel memories of your ancestors in your body?*

# CHAPTER 10

## *The Tree of Knowledge and Spirituality*

### Alexandra The Past

In San Francisco, 1969, I celebrated my fifteenth birthday, to the music of the Beatles and the wisdom of *Siddhartha* by Hermann Hesse. George Harrison inspired me to meditate and learn about yoga. Siddhartha lit the light of my soul to search for truth. I welcomed the teachings of mysticism from many sources.

I found a small and unassuming pamphlet on my mother's bedside table. It talked about God in a different way, saying that there was order in the universe and science gave us an understanding of that order. It showed a triangle and described its connection to the divine power of the universe. What moved me most was a picture of a man's face with light emitting from his forehead. I had learned in yoga that this was the third eye, the place of perception or clairvoyance. As I finished reading the pamphlet, I felt something shifting inside of me. I knew this was something important and that I had to learn more about it.

When my mother came home from work, I asked her about it. She said a friend had recommended it to her so she could become more psychic. It was a home study program, and she would share it with me.

When the material arrived, my mother became very secretive and would not share it with me. After a few weeks she said the exercises had scared her and she would not be continuing her program. I asked her if I could study her material. She said no, but if I was really interested, she would help me pay for them. I said yes immediately.

For the next three years I studied these materials, which were from the Rosicrucian Order. This was a Tree of Knowledge that changed my life forever. I learned many valuable and sacred teachings about our existence. One of the greatest lessons I learned was that we are all connected by a universal powerful force or God.

As I turned sixteen, I was able to get my driver's license. I became the designated driver for family errands. On occasion I drove my mother and her girlfriends to nightclubs. They would have fun, drink, and dance, and I would drive them all safely home.

On one of these nights I drove my mother and her girlfriends out to a couple of Latin clubs in the Mission District of San Francisco. On our way home my mother became argumentative because she'd had too much to drink and wanted to drive home herself. I would not let her, so she told me to get out of the car. It was 1:30 in the morning as I got out on the corner of 30$^{th}$ and Mission. Known as the Upper Mission, it is where the night clubbers go to eat after dancing and drinking. Authentic Mexican and Central American food is served in a handful of meager-looking restaurants. By this time of night the fog was rolling in, providing panhandlers a hidden resting place for the night.

I saw a gasoline station and walked over, thinking I could use their phone. I spoke to the gasoline attendant and told him my dilemma. I wanted to call my grandmother and ask her to help me pay for a cab when I got home. He said sure and pointed to where the office phone was. As I was walking toward the office, a couple in a blue pickup truck called out to me to come over to them. They were Hispanic, and the woman said they had heard my story as I was talking to the attendant. They offered to help me out by taking me home at no charge, so I got into the pickup truck.

I told them where I lived, and the woman said she needed to get home first but her nephew, who was driving, would take me. We dropped her off at her house on 24th Street and headed for Highway 280 toward Daly City. The man driving me was in his early twenties, slender with black hair and eyes. He was quiet, so I was very surprised when he asked, "Do you have any marijuana on you?"

I said, "No, I don't smoke that stuff."

He said, "Sure you do," and then he put his hand on my knee.

I shoved his hand off my knee and wrenched my legs away. He laughed and said, "Tonight I am going to rape you." He sped up the truck and took the Junipero Serra Blvd. exit. I knew I was in danger, and I had to do something quickly. I thought of my grandmother, Papa Roberto, and God, the triangle. I began praying inside. I invoked the presence of God and His power of protection.

In the middle of all the fog the signal light turned a bright red. The car came to a screeching halt. An enormous brilliant ball of light exploded between the driver and me. It was so bright that I could no longer see him. An arrow of light flung the truck door open to my right, and another explosion of light pushed me out of the car. I fell to the ground. All I could see were the tires in front of my eyes. Everything had stopped. A voice inside of me said, "Take off your shoes and run. Do not stop until I tell you."

Quickly I did what I was told—a spiritual lesson put into practice at a moment's notice.

I ran and ran into the fog of Daly City. The truck made a U-turn and came after me. When I saw this, the voice kept saying, "Run, run, run, run." I do not know how long I ran. Then the voice said, "Stop. They are coming." I saw lights coming through the fog. It was a police car. They pulled over and came to my rescue. One officer came out of the car and cautiously walked toward me. I was so full of relief, and as I pointed to the truck, it roared, and then the fog swallowed it up. Out of breath, I quickly told the officer what had happened. He gently put me in the backseat of the car and drove to the local Lyons Restaurant a few blocks away. As they parked the car, the feelings of what had happened began to come over me. I started to cry, and my body began to shake.

The officers asked for my home address and phone number. One police officer made a call, giving all my information. Soon we could hear through the dispatch that someone had tried calling my home and reached my grandmother, who responded in a few uncomprehending Spanish words. They drove me home. When we arrived, my grandmother was waiting. Within minutes my mother pulled into the driveway. She had been crying. She said that she had gone back to pick me up after the argument but could not find me. Before the police officers left, they told my mother, "Your daughter is very lucky to be alive." While my mother thanked the officers and closed the door, my grandmother held me in her arms. Then she took my hand and safely tucked me into bed. I told her in detail what had happened. She became lost in thought when I told her about the explosion of light. This was the beginning of my sojourn with the healing light of God. It anchored the knowing that I was not alone.

My grandmother kissed my forehead and said, "I knew something was wrong. I have been praying all night. No more driving at this hour ever again. I will tell your mother." I heard her go into my mother's bedroom. The sound of my grandmother's voice was like a whip cutting through my mother's sobs. The last words split the door open and shut. My grandmother went to bed. Her force moved the evening, ending it in a peaceful place.

I woke up to the aroma of my favorite breakfast, the Salvadorean sweet cake called quesadilla and *café con leche* (milk with coffee). The morning gave me my loving grandmother, who was waiting for me in the kitchen.

**Spirit asks: Have you ever been protected from harm by God?**

# CHAPTER 11

## *The Cemetery*

**Alexandra The Past**

The Mission District of San Francisco held the hidden village of Santeria or "Healing Magic." Now this can mean many things. It always depended on what you needed it for. My mother needed healing magic to get my father back home and be faithful to her. The cures or magic potions she purchased did not last very long. They must have had an expiration date.

My mother was always looking for a new place to go, hoping that this time it would work. She always brought me along because I could tell if these *santeros* (shamans/healers/curanderos) were real. Many people here called themselves santeros, but they were not. They pretended to be, only for the money. I had the radar. I could scan their energy field, and I would know. If I saw lights around the santero, I knew spirits were coming in to help. The energy must be strong like a magnet and the colors bright and pure. My mother trusted me.

My father had been gone for a month without a word, and my mother had become very desperate. A friend of hers had recommended a powerful *santera*. So we made our journey down to La Mission. It was late afternoon when we arrived. I did not like the santera the moment I saw her. She was small with little black pearly eyes that held you when she looked at you. She had a red silk scarf like a turban around her head, and she wore a long white dress. Around her neck hung colorful beaded necklaces and then a very large wooden cross, a crucifix. I became alarmed when I saw Jesus was missing. She took us to a room filled with candles and pictures of people I did not recognize. They were not saints. That should have been a big warning.

The santera knew why my mother was there because they'd talked on the phone when my mom made the appointment. The santera told my mother that she would give her a very powerful incantation and potion. It would cost her $200.00. My mother did not flinch, but I did as I watched the santera take the money and put inside her bra. I asked myself, "Who is this woman?" I scanned her energy. She emitted a strong energy field that was real, but I saw no sparkling lights around her. Another warning.

She prepared a potion in a regular glass honey jar. She said incoherent words and blew them into the jar where the honey caught them. She poured herbs by pinching them as they fell in pain. At last she handed the jar to my mother along with two black candles each in a glass container. She sternly held my mother's attention and said the following, "You are to go to the cemetery nearest you and find a grave with a woman's name ... any woman on it. The grave should be in a mausoleum so the candle does not blow out. Pour half of this mixture in front or over the grave and light the candle. Call out her name and tell her she is to serve you. Then go home, light the other candle, and pour the rest of the mixture where your husband sleeps." I shuddered, and my mother looked at me without saying a word except, *"Gracias."*

We left and drove to the cemetery. I was completely shaken, knowing that this was wrong. We were not working with the light of God. We were activating dark forces to do our bidding. This did not stop my mother. All she could think of was getting my father back. She was willing to pay any price.

We ended up at Holy Cross Cemetery in South San Francisco as the sun was setting. My mother was on a mission, and she quickly found the spot. It was a dark gray mausoleum with an iron gate that easily opened. We went down a few steps and found a woman's name. My mother lit the candle, invoked the woman's name, and commanded her service as she poured half the mixture over the grave site. We swiftly left as the last rays of light disappeared. I told her this ritual made me feel afraid. I knew God would not want us to do this. She ignored my words and said, "You are only here to help me."

We drove home, and I went straight to my room. I lay on my bed and closed my eyes. I saw images of swirling darkness. A commanding voice said, "Stop this now." I jumped off the bed and ran to my mother's bedroom, where I found her reading a book. I saw the black candle lit and the rest of the mixture poured on the bed where my father slept.

I looked at my mom and said, "We are going to stop this. If we continue, it will harm our family for generations to come. Your grandchildren, my children." She looked up at me, exhausted, and I felt her energy fading. She said, "Okay, *esta bien* (it is all right). Do what you need to do."

As my mother got off the bed, I quickly pulled the bed sheets off and blew out the candle. I went to the kitchen and got all the salt we had and ran outside, pouring the salt around the house. In the backyard I cut six roses to represent the sacred Trinity and brought them into my mother's bedroom. I placed three roses next to the picture of the Blessed Mother. I woke up my grandmother and told her what had happened. I asked her to start praying and said we needed to ask for forgiveness for what we had just done.

I looked at my mother and said, "Come with me."

We drove back to the cemetery, carrying salt, the remaining three roses, and some of my grandmother's holy water. It was dark, but we found the mausoleum and quickly blew out the candle. We starting praying and asked Jesus to forgive and help us. For me it was spooky to see my mother frozen and withdrawn as if she had become a ghost. I sprinkled the salt first. Next I poured the holy water over the grave and spread the rose petals upon it. Then we left.

On our way home my mother started to cry. She was confused by what had happened. I became very serious. I spoke to her as if she were a child and said, "I will never go with you again to any of these Santeria places. This was wrong, and it is not the way to get my father back home. Great harm could have come to our family. You need to accept the fact that my dad likes to be with other women. He will come home when he is tired and needs rest. You nicknamed him El Cometa (the comet), which explains his erratic family appearances perfectly."

My mother said nothing. I knew she did not agree with me. It did not matter. I never went again.

For me this was an important turning point of my life. I had made a conscious moral decision to engage in truth and only work with God's light. Decades later I believe that this decision allowed me to see and talk to David the way that I do now. I am in gratitude for God's grace and benevolence.

**Spirit asks: Do you believe that there are different forces in the Spirit world, and that some are not benevolent towards us?**

## *Ode on Intimations of Immortality-continued*

Thou, whose exterior semblance doth believe
Thy soul's immensity;
thou best philosopher, who yet dost keep
Thy heritage, thou eye among the blind,
That, deaf and silent, read'st the eternal deep,
Haunted for ever by the eternal mind,
Mighty prophet! Seer blest!
On whom those truths do rest,
Which we are toiling all our lives to find—

—William Wordsworth

# CHAPTER 12

## Medicine Wheel

*The gap of time intensified when I physically left. You remained in a time capsule. The light of me went into a race of lights as I soared into an incredible energy field and became one again.*
—David (communication received in a meditation)

### Alexandra, November 1992

Who is to say where life resides? Life gives birth to the soul through the womb. When the soul is released from the body, it returns to its place of origin: life in God.

Many traditions honor this mystery. David's passing was honored a few months later in the fall. November held the crisp air at bay. In the small California town of Sebastopol, Daphne, a friend of many years, and her husband, Frank, gathered my sisterhood and friends of the heart. She asked Chauntra Windwalker, a Shaman from Arizona, to do a special healing ritual and activate the medicine wheel behind Daphne's home.

The medicine wheel comes from Native American traditions.

This is a wheel of healing energy releasing its power to those inside its circle. Stones are strategically placed in a circle, and the elements of water, fire, wood, and metal mark the four directions- north, east, south, and west- with candles. On this particular day Chauntra placed a big quartz crystal about 12 inches long in the center of the medicine wheel. Daphne had a picture of David next to the crystal, and lit a white candle. Chauntra would be activating the medicine wheel by calling forth the ancestors of the land and the totem or medicine animals associated with each of the four directions.

Here is what happened, what stays with me: The ritual began when we were all gathered. Twenty-seven women and men came to partake in this special Native American ritual that honored David's transition and my grief as his mother. Chauntra was dressed in an aqua blue suede top with dark pants with a beautiful silver necklace that held turquoise stones in place. She wore a straw hat underneath a headdress with white and brown feathers. In her right hand she held a peace pipe. Her sparkling eyes matched the color of the turquoise stones. She chose those who would assist in the process, and the sound of the drums surrounded us. We all stood in line a few feet from the medicine wheel. Its circular size was about twenty feet as it rested in the middle of a grove surrounded by oak trees. We were all given white feathers to hold and small bundles of tobacco wrapped in white cloth with a turquoise ribbon binding it.

Before we entered the medicine wheel, Cherie (Daphne's niece) began purifying and clearing our bodies with sage, a medicinal herb that is burned in a shell. (A white feather is used to move the smoke around the body. This helps clear negative energies and bring balance to the physical and aura fields.) We were then prepared to enter the medicine wheel clockwise. We moved to the rhythm of drums playing. I was guided to the center of the medicine wheel as I held in my arms David's favorite teddy bear, his blue jacket, and his baby blanket.

Chauntra's thunderous voice invoked the four directions, moving us all to face each direction as it was called. Her voice moved like the wind as she said, "I open up the gateway of the north, the east, the south, and the west."

As she did this, we could hear the strong heartbeat of twin drums playing. Their sounds moved through us, making us vibrate at a higher level of awareness. This is the medicine of sound that heals.

Chauntra stood in the center of the circle and took the small white rabbit skin from the altar. Moving clockwise, she placed the white rabbit skin in front of the first person. I went around the circle, standing before each person. We knelt down on the rabbit skin, facing each other. Looking into each other's eyes, heart to heart, each person gave me a verbal blessing. The tobacco bundles held the blessing energetically, and each person gave me a bundle to keep. Then Chauntra took all the bundles, put them in a sand-colored suede pouch, and had me carry it over my shoulders.

I was then invited and allowed to express my grief vocally. I knew I was safe to do this because as I looked at everyone's face, I could feel love and compassion reaching out to me. I wrapped the arms of David's jacket around me. I began to let the moaning pain rise up. I revealed my wound, and its sound rapidly came roaring out. Agony reverberated through my body. I felt myself gasping with death and parched with life. As I started looking at everyone again, I realized that David was there. He was witnessing the entire experience outside the circle. Chauntra and others acknowledged his presence. Throughout the rest of the ceremony David was with us.

Chauntra started playing the windpipe. Its healing sound wrapped around us like a ribbon connecting each of us together. Then the chanting began. I heard vibrant Indian words that my mind could not understand, but my body did. Everyone held out their hands, sending energy into the crystal and me. The wind began to blow heavy sighs. The sun was at its highest, bright and hot. Energy began spinning all around us as the beating of the drums grew louder and more rhythmic. My body began to spin as well, and then I felt I was being lifted, as if I was floating a few inches in the air. I don't remember how long it lasted. It seemed endless, and I did not want it to stop. I wanted to keep floating higher and higher until I could reach the heavens and be with my David.

My circle of women and men continued holding their hands up, facing me, which generated love, love from my sisterhood and brotherhood that created a spiritual vortex. When my feet felt the ground again, the sensation of touching the earth was light, as if my feet were on a cloud. This spiritual vortex of love and light energy began to fill the wound in my heart and soul.

A special healing had been given to me.

As the months passed, I discovered the transformations of my soul. At times I was peaceful, and I could surrender to all that had happened. At other times I was an angry mother who was distraught that something so unfair had been thrust onto her.

I felt the waves crashing into each other. I was aware.

*Spirit asks: Do you believe that there is a Mother Earth that has the power to heal you? Does she have medicine for you? Do you honor her gifts, take care of her, and teach your children why?*

The medicine wheel ritual, as I kneeled in front of each person to receive their blessing (November 1992).

# CHAPTER 13

## *Grieving*

*I am evolving as you do. Thank you for always including me in your life. I am loved and remembered through you.*
—David (communication received in a meditation)

### Alexandra 1993

It is the beginning of the new year. January 1993 begins my first year without my David. I don't know how I will handle his seventh birthday on May 11. He was born on Mother's Day. What will happen to me on this Mother's Day or any other holiday? No Valentine Day card in February. My birthday is in a few weeks, and who will give me a birthday card signed David? I want to see his handwriting and special drawings.

The pain comes in waves. I am afraid of what will happen when these special dates arrive, so I cry in waves of agony. Holidays arrive, and I freeze up. In the weeks that follow, the waves of sadness leave me dry of all emotions.

I am told by friends that I need to let him go. What in the hell does that mean? He was taken away from me. I had no choice in the matter. He is physically gone. I remind myself of the miracles that I have experienced, and it is not enough. It will never be enough.

I remember something so devastating that I could not articulate when it happened. My friend Roni wanted to help me clean up my home. I agreed because I saw that she really wanted to help me and frankly I did not care what my apartment looked like.

What she did was clean out David's room. She put his things in bags. She threw out what looked like junk to her. When I walked into his room, his things were not there. I went into shock. When I could speak, I asked her why she had removed everything. Roni said she felt that it would be easier to get on with my grieving if I was not reminded of David. Wipe the slate clean. He no longer exists. No need to be reminded. I have heard similar stories of parents being put through this by family or friends. I was so outraged that I slammed the emotional door on Roni and never wanted to see her again. Our friendship ended.

I retrieved what I could from the dumpster. A little piece of gum with his teeth marks on it is my treasure. I bought two long storage boxes for his toys, clothes, drawings, and things that could only be important to me. They both fit perfectly under my bed. All for me! To look at whenever I want to. David's things comforted me, a collection of sweet memories, his footprints in the sand. I was also aware that when I cry too much and long for him, he feels my sadness. As a grieving mother it was difficult to hear that I should let go of my child, but David showed me that for now he was with me. I was learning to accept this new way of life. My existence had become surreal, filled with hope, sadness, and miracles.

Finally I decided to go to the Contra Costa Bereaved Family and Support Center. Meetings were every Thursday night at 7:30. It took five minutes to drive there. The room was filled with about ten couples and another eight like me who had come alone. We sat in a circle with a licensed therapist guiding the session. Each of us shared our personal story. We learned that it does not matter if your child died of an illness or an accident. We are never prepared for what will happen. It is okay to grieve for as long as you need to. Who made up the rule to get over it and move on? Obviously it was not a bereaved parent.

About a month later I started to see flickering lights around some of the parents. These lights were very similar to David's. I soon realized that these lights were the energy fields of the children that had come to visit their parents.

Telling our stories can be very emotional, both for the ones sharing as well as those who are listening, as we only speak when we are moved to. I started to hear a few telepathic messages from some of the visiting children. At first I did not know what to do. Then I started sharing some of my spiritual experiences with David. If parents approached me afterward and shared that they sometimes felt or sensed their children, I would open up and give them their message.

One of the patterns that I discovered in the grieving process was that women were more receptive to what I had to say. As women we grieve in the moment. We expose our loss immediately because we are used to expressing all our feelings. It is what we do. The men I encountered were usually stoic in holding themselves together for the whole family, protecting the family until they are safe. In our gatherings it was over a year before I saw fathers completely express their grief.

There was a particular couple that had difficulty hearing what I had to say. Their child had made his transition about five years earlier. He was twenty-five years old and had passed away because of an illness. They came every Thursday and shared their pain and the dreams they had had for him. One day the mom came to me as were walking out to the parking lot. She said, "You are the only one who will understand this. When I walk our dog, just ahead of me I sometimes see my son. He is wearing his favorite red cap. I see him only for an instant. He turns and smiles and then disappears. My husband thinks I am going crazy. Am I?"

I looked deeply into her eyes. Holding both of her hands, I said, "No, they never leave us. He is joining you for a walk with the dog, and he is happy. That is why he is smiling. You saw your son, and I think we all are a little crazy after all we have gone through. You have received a miracle. Be grateful to God and continue walking with your son. It is your time together." I held her in my arms. We cried.

As I drove away, I heard a lovely voice say to me, "Thank you for taking care of my mother."

It is hard to understand all the emotions that run through you at once. I did not listen to music for over a year. Music is a form of celebration, and I had nothing to celebrate. Terrible news was worth hearing. Could things be worse in the world than my situation? Somehow I was hoping they were.

The tragedy is that as parents many of us do blame ourselves. I go over and over the details of the day that took my son away. I create all the different ways in which I could have prevented it. As a mother I found it very hard to forgive myself for not preventing the death of my son. My mind became prolific in tracking the moments of conversation I could have had with him. Could I have changed his destiny if I had been there with him or made sure that he was in school all day? If I had chosen another place to live and work, would it have made a difference? If the paramedics had arrived earlier or if he had gone to a different hospital, would he still be alive? I went over all the what-ifs with a fine-tooth comb. How much does karma and free will influence the choices we make? I ponder this mystery. I do not know. *If only* is the common theme in my mind. With time I can say we do become brave. We have experienced the worst thing that could happen to parents, and we survived it. At least most of us do, to some degree. Everything else in life is manageable. Nothing compares to it. We can handle anything. Therein lies our bravery.

In my support group I once said, "Show me the doorway that leads out of here. I will gladly go anytime." Everyone looked at me and agreed. Me, the spiritual one, looking for a way out! Yes, the yearning to be with your child takes over.

Did God have a plan? To this day I say I have a divine appointment with God so he can explain to me how all of this was for my good. Did I have a spiritual agreement with David to experience this? It took me a long time to finally say yes. It happened because the miracles kept coming. One in particular began in my support group, and played itself out in my future.

A bereaved mother came in from another group, with her husband. She shared their sad story of her daughter's accidental death. Her husband was the stepfather, very withdrawn and quiet, and the stress was ending their marriage. I would run into her at other gatherings. We discovered we had friends in common. We would greet each other, but her pain became her shield of protection. In time I lost track of her.

Years later in the spring of 1999 I met my future husband, Richard. As we dated, the Fourth of July weekend came upon us. We decided to have a picnic and share some of our history. Richard said he wanted to tell me a very deep and sad story in his life. He had been married a few years before, and his ex-wife had had a daughter whom he had loved very much. He had taken her to a school event at Ocean Beach in San Francisco. She went walking on the cliffs with some friends. She accidently slipped and fell into the ocean. They were never able to find her body.

I was already crying by the time he finished sharing his story. I knew this had been the stepfather from the bereavement support group. We looked into each other's eyes, and I told him what I was remembering. We held each other and cried for each other's loss. We realized that God had brought us together.

*Spirit asks: Are we a spiritual family? Do you believe we have met each other in heaven, and we continue our journey here on earth? Is everyone we meet significant?*

# CHAPTER 15

## My Daughter, Amira, Arrives

> *Guardian Angels celebrate when a soul is birthed on earth, they look forward to the sacred journey together.*
> —Spirit (communication received in a meditation)

### Alexandra 1993

Getting pregnant after David's passing saved my life. The November following the accident, in the midst of my turmoil with my husband of that time, I felt life stirring inside of me. It became my hope that life would go on and that I could survive what had happened.

Before my pregnancy, to die in an automobile accident had been my wish. I had decided to make it happen so I could follow David in the same way he had left. Strange, unforeseen things started to happen. It began with a few flat tires while I was driving. Then brakes failed. Cars honked at me when I crossed over to a new lane. It seemed as if my desire to be with David was going to be fulfilled. Signal lights would turn red while I was crossing the intersection. I had not seen the yellow light. It was obvious to me that something was going to happen soon.

Carrying a child turned everything around for me. I had to remain here and give birth to a new life. The desire to leave ended, and I embraced that new life. Could the baby be the reincarnation of David? Yes, I thought about that. I waited for the spiritual signs to appear.

I was concerned that the baby inside of me would be affected by and possibly absorb my grief. I wanted my baby to be happy and emotionally healthy. I decided to look for a massage therapist that could help me with this. I made a plea to God to connect me with a healer.

I thought of going back to Maria, but it was difficult to find her, which I took as a sign that she was not the one for me now. I had met Maria about a month after David's transition. I was taken to a healing center by one of my sisters, who made appointments for my mother and me to help us with our grieving. I remember asking for a female massage therapist, and soon a small vibrant woman appeared. She had short black hair and striking blue eyes. Her name was Maria. She guided me to a quiet room where soft harp music was playing. She had placed a blue silk scarf over the lamp shade, which gave it a heavenly glow. She explained what I needed to do, and then she asked me to pick a tarot card. I was a little surprised, but I went ahead and picked one. The card I choose was the death card. Maria did not flinch. She took the card, put it on her altar, and lit a candle.

She said, "This card is about transformation, life and death. It is the same experience."

I was stunned and did not say anything. I had come here to relax and let things go for a while. This was not what I was expecting to happen. Maria left the room. I got undressed and slipped into the massage table as she had instructed. Soon I heard a soft knock on the door, and she came in.

Maria began her massage, and I could feel a lot of warm energy flowing from her hands. I knew she was a healer. After about ten minutes went by, she said, "We have a visitor. Is it okay if I tell you who it is?"

I could hardly speak but managed to say, "Yes."

"He says he is your son. He looks young and is very excited about communicating with you this way."

Painful tears started to flow out of me.

"Yes," I said again, "please tell me what he is saying."

"He wants you to know he is with you all the time, that he loves you very much, and to try not to be so sad. When things get difficult for you, he will be there. You will feel his hand touching your right hand. He also says his sister is coming."

I could hear Maria's voice choking up. I looked up at her and saw that she was crying.

"He is so beautiful. His love for you radiates like a beam of light illuminating this whole room."

Maria gently placed her hands around my shoulders, holding me until I could stop crying. Soon she was able to continue and finish her healing massage. I saw Maria a few more times. Each time was just as prophetic. I will never forget what she channeled and the comfort it gave me.

I began my quest for another massage therapist by going to Dolphin Dreams, my favorite metaphysical bookstore in Walnut Creek. They had a newsletter, which I took home and carefully read through. I saw a small ad that held my attention. It had an angel with the name Kathy on it. I immediately called her. Kathy answered the phone, and I explained my situation to her. I asked if she could help me heal some of my pain so that my baby would not absorb my grief. She listened, and in a kind voice explained the type of massage and healing work she believed could help me. I felt a connection with her, so I made a massage appointment for

Thursday in the morning, the same day of my bereaved parent support group. I drove to Danville and arrived at the Rose Street Center. As soon as we met, we immediately liked each other. Kathy was moved by my story. I went to her once a week for nine months.

During this time Kathy had several extraordinary experiences with David. The most memorable one took place in her garden. Kathy meditated in her garden every morning to help her prepare for the day. On this particular Thursday morning David appeared to her. He thanked her for taking care of me. He wanted me to know that he was with his baby sister. He said he was telling her all about the family and things that were important for her to know. Kathy described him, and then she said he had Buddha energy. As always, the miracle astounded me. I told Kathy that I would sometimes call him the Little Buddha because he was so wise and he had a peaceful energy around him.

When my daughter, Amira, was born, Kathy came to visit me. She had a special gift for my infant daughter. It was a beautiful delicate amethyst crystal on a gold chain. It was the perfect size for Amira. A crystal amethyst has a very high vibration. It is in the vibration of healing, and it helps connect us with the wise teacher within, also referred to as the Christ light or the Buddha of the heart. I looked into Kathy's beautiful brown eyes and acknowledged the meaning held in her gift.

We went to the nursery. I picked up Amira and handed her over to Kathy. As soon as she heard Kathy's voice, she opened her eyes and reached for her finger. She would not let go. We were both amazed that the baby had recognized her so quickly. Frankly it made sense. After nine months of incredible healing massages, of course my daughter would recognize her massage therapist. I have very sweet memories of my tummy being massaged and the baby responding to Kathy's healing touch. My daughter was born emotionally healthy. As a baby she had a sweet, mellow quality about her. As she has grown up, remaining calm in stressful situations is her strength. Kathy and I have remained friends, periodically meeting for lunch and catching up.

During the time that I was getting massages, I asked Kathy how she had become a massage therapist. She told me where she had gone but said there was school in Walnut Creek run by a blind woman named Nancy Burr. The seed was planted. I decided I wanted to become a massage therapist so that I could help heal people who were grieving. It had helped me so much that I wanted to give it back. I knew that it worked, and I wanted to learn how.

Yes, God had a plan. I was being prepared to enter into a new phase of my life as a spiritual massage therapist.

***Spirit asks: Do you believe we all have guardian angels or guides, who create synchronicity and miracles to remind us that we are never alone?***

# CHAPTER 15

## *Happy Birthday, David*

> *Validating a spiritual experience is being of service, both to God and mankind.*
> —Alexandra

### Alexandra May 1993

Becoming a certified massage therapist was the most natural thing that I could do. I jumped right into it. When I graduated, I was offered a teaching job at the American Institute of Massage in Walnut Creek, my massage school. Like most massage therapists, I also started working out of my home. After a few months I rented a space at the Rose Street Center in Danville. This was the same place that Kathy, my massage therapist, worked out of. What a gift to be able to give healing treatments where I had received so my much of that myself! The cycle of life had come full circle again. It was here that I met Stacy, another massage therapist who was very intuitive and had the healing touch. We shared the same treatment room but on different days.

David's birthday was only a few days away, May 11. This is the day that David always gives me a miracle. I shared my story with Stacy, but I had not told her that his birthday would be soon.

On May 11 Stacy stopped by to give me a special gift, a flower. She said she had been running errands earlier in downtown Walnut Creek. As she was passing a flower shop, she felt a presence. Stacy heard a voice that said to her, "Please buy a flower for my mom today. I want her to know that I am thinking of her like she is thinking of me." Stacy said she knew she had to do it because it could only be David making this request.

She walked into the flower shop. David started to communicate with her again. He told her what flower to buy, and she did it without hesitation.

When she came to our healing center, she quickly found me and sat me down. "This is from David. He picked the flower and asked me to tell you he is thinking of you like you are thinking of him," she said.

It was a delicate light lavender rose in a cellophane wrap. The petals were round, and it had a hint of white and pink. The rose had a short stem with few tiny green leaves. I had never seen a beautiful flower like this. It had a familiar fragrance, almost like a gardenia but softer. *Why did David pick this particular flower?* I asked myself.

Stacy intuitively answered my question. "The name of the rose is angel face," she said quickly.

"Oh, my God, David's birthday miracle! This is what I always called him, angel face. That's why he picked this flower." My voice boomed with excitement.

Stacy and I hugged, mesmerized by the miracle.

Every year on May 11 David gives me a birthday surprise. Also every year on August 14, the day of David's transition, something special happens. It comes in the form of an answer to a problem, or a surprise moment that reminds me David is with me.

***Spirit asks: When have you felt part of a chain of miracles?***

# CHAPTER 16

## *The Healing World of Massage*

> *Healers are messengers of God.*
> —Alexandra

### Alexandra September 1993

Nestled in the Berkley Hills is a glowing white Victorian castle that looks like a painting by Maxfield Parrish. It is called the Claremont Hotel and Spa. Working in a beautiful environment was the perfect time to use my massage skills as a healer. I had come to understand that the grief I carried in my heart seemed to attract clients who were also grieving.

It so happened that one day I had a client named Joan. (I have changed her name to protect her privacy.) As I started to massage her, she began to quietly sob. I continued and asked her if she was okay. Joan started to tell me her story. Her husband had passed away several months before, and she was grieving his death and other things that had recently happened to her.

I asked her if she felt her husband around her or in her dreams.

She said she could smell him in their bedroom. In her dreams she would have conversations with him. He was telling her to continue her life and that it was fine to meet someone else and fall in love again. This made her very sad, and she would wake up crying. After these dreams she missed him even more. As she was talking, I started to see beautiful white sparkly lights entering the room. These lights looked like very small orbs and lingered near my client. I knew it was a being of light, and I assumed it was her husband. With my inner voice, I asked the light who it was, and it said, "My name is Mark."

Very carefully, I told Joan that I was a clairvoyant and that at times when giving massages, I would get messages. I asked if she was comfortable receiving some information. She lifted her head out of the face cradle and said yes, because she had been praying for something very important.

I then said, "I believe this is your husband, Mark. He wants me to tell you that he is here."

Joan froze and said, "This is unbelievable. I know a Mark, but he is not my husband. Mark was the first love of my life, and I have been praying to reconnect with him. I have tried many ways of finding him but no luck."

I looked at the sparkling light and said, "Mark, what is your message to Joan? You have our complete attention."

Mark said, "Tell Joan I passed away four years ago. I moved to Louisiana, and I am buried in Morgan City. My mother and brother still live there. She will find me there, but it really is not important. Tell her that what is important is that I remember her with my soul, and if I was alive, I would marry her and live out the life we had always dreamed of."

I felt very overwhelmed, and asked him to help me tell her. This was a lot of information, and I needed to be careful about how much to say.

I turned Joan over on her back and began massaging her neck and shoulder. Then I said, "Mark has a lot of important things to share with you. That he is in spirit form tells us he has made his transition."

"I was afraid of that," Joan said, wiping her tears away.

I then proceeded to tell her what Mark had said. She took it all in, and I finished her massage, helped her sit up and asked her if she had any questions for Mark. She said yes. This was Joan's question: Had Mark made contact with her husband, Tom? I looked over where Mark was standing, and I asked telepathically, "Mark, you heard Joan's question. Have you seen Tom?"

Mark said, "No, I have not seen him." I shared this with Joan.

Joan said, "Mark, I love you, and I am so sorry we never saw each other again. We were so young."

Mark's light moved closer to Joan, surrounding her. I saw her body go limp as she surrendered to this light. She was filled with love. Tenderly the light disappeared, and Joan looked up at me.

She said, "I could feel that. I am so relieved. I had been praying to God to help me find Mark, and so He did. I know now why I came here today. It was not for a massage, but for you to help me put closure to Mark and remove the pressure of trying to find him. Thank you for helping me. You are my messenger. I will never forget you."

Joan gave me a soothing hug, and I walked her back to her dressing room. Back in my room, I did some Reiki to reinforce the energy of healing. I thanked Mark for coming and made sure the room was clear of any emotional energy that needed to be released. I said a special prayer of gratitude to God for allowing this miracle to happen. This was the beginning of many healings of this nature. I felt blessed to be of service.

These healings included strangers as well as friends I knew. I had a dear friend named Hilda who became my client. She was also a massage therapist and had been suffering from lower back pain. She made an appointment and came to see me the following day. Knowing that her main concern was her lower back, I knew that meant that she was in a lot of emotional stress because of some kind of trauma. I began my massage. I felt the energy stuck in the tailbone. I let Hilda know and placed both my hands over it. I visualized Reiki symbols, Dr. Usui's method of healing the body, over this area, and we both could feel the energy begin to move.

Suddenly I started to see an image forming itself in the tailbone. I did not see this with my eyes open. It was inner sight. I saw a baby curled up inside the tailbone, and it was crying and screaming. I just kept sending it energy with my hands. As a healer it is very important to remove all judgment so the energy can move freely, and this is what I did. I finally decided to tell Hilda. As I did, she started to cry very deeply. I stopped massaging her and gave her some water and tissue paper. When she felt calmer, she told me her daughter, who had recently turned twenty-one, had just moved out of the house for the first time, and she was missing her terribly. She wanted her baby back. Hilda was worried that if her daughter needed help, she might not be able to reach her. She had stopped herself from calling her every day. She was in fear of losing her only child, her baby. This is what she was carrying in her lower back.

The energy that flows through me is from God. It has universal thought and holds all answers. I was being guided to release the energy of fear and in its place establish trust. I asked Hilda, "Are you ready to let go of your fear of losing your daughter?"

She said, "Yes, I am."

Then I said, "We ask God and all his angels of light to give you the energy of trust and safety. Let it be established in the tailbone, your lower back, and anywhere else you need it. This is done through the power of God's love, and so it is." I channeled this energy until it released me like a magnet letting go. It lasted about ten minutes. I never know how long it will take.

Hilda's breath started to change, as usually the life force in the breath calms and releases. When I finished, I told Hilda to take her time and to let me know when she was ready to get up. I always help my clients up after these healings because sometimes the energy is so powerful that they might feel dizzy. About fifteen minutes later Hilda called out to me, letting me know she was ready. I came in, and she was glowing. She said she felt relieved and the tension had left her body. I could feel and see that something good had happened.

A few months after Hilda's healing, she met a good man. I received an invitation to their wedding. Hilda had been a widow for many years and had been very afraid of dating. With the fear gone, many loving things happened.

As for Hilda's daughter, she also got married. Hilda is now a happy grandmother enjoying her time with a new baby girl in her arms.

**Spirit asks: Do you believe in the power of healing? How do you experience it in your life?**

# CHAPTER 17

## *David's Second Birthday in Heaven*

*Down in the valley the valley so low, angels in heaven know I love you, you, you, singing helps heal the heart.*
—Alexandra

### Alexandra

On May 11, 1994, I woke up thinking, *How will David celebrate his second birthday in heaven? Will he have a birthday cake? Who will bake it? Who will be invited?* I closed my eyes, trying to see what it would look like. *Oh, God, please make his birthday in heaven happy and beautiful so he does not miss his family and me.* I had resolved this year to have a birthday party for David. It was still important to celebrate the day of his birth. I wanted to disregard the usual family hush when a child is no longer living. God would take care of it in heaven, and I would take care of it here. I invited his cousins to celebrate him and share their favorite David stories as their gifts.

I had baked David his favorite chocolate cake. I put a few brightly colored balloons in the dining room. I had Batman, his favorite comic book character, paper plates and napkins on the table. Everything looked ready. I was happy, sad, excited, and full of expectation to be with David's cousins again for this occasion.

David now had a baby sister, Amira, who on his birthday was ten months old. That morning I could hear her giggling in her room as if she was talking to someone. I quietly opened the door. She was looking up, trying to touch something with her hands. Then I started to see sparks of blue lights. Yes, something was moving above her. It was a lovely silhouette of waves of light. Amira's face glowed with happiness. I knew it was David. He had joined us for his birthday celebration. I gently closed the door. Both my children were home.

I heard a knock on the door. I quickly looked around the living room, making sure all three surprise treat bags were still there. I opened the door, and there stood David's cousins Michael, Nicole, and Brian, with shy smiles, but smiles, to my relief.

Behind them stood my cousin's wife, Monique, the mother of Michael and Nicole. We hugged and kissed as they came in. They were excited to see Amira, so we went to her bedroom. As I stood there and watched them, I felt a relief that we were all together. I picked up Amira, and we all went into the living room.

I gave the children their treat bags full of candy and small toys. As they smiled, we began telling David stories. We laughed and cried a little, and then we sang "Happy Birthday" to David. I served them cake and ice cream. Soon after, they wanted to play in David's bedroom. I took them all into his room and left them there to play with his toys while Monique and I chatted in the living room. I was expressing my gratitude to her for bringing the children and making it feel so normal. When they came out and joined us, we could both feel their sadness, so we knew they were missing David.

We were startled when Amira came crawling out behind them and suddenly stood up. She looked at her cousins and said, "Paco, Cole, Rian." We were astounded. These were the nicknames that David had given his cousins. I then remembered that Amira had been playing with David earlier. I believe he told her to use their nicknames. We all realized we had just experienced a David miracle. This moment was filled with love, awe, and joy because we all shared it.

When we sat down again, Monique handed me a small plump album full of David pictures. We hugged, embracing the memories we shared.

Monique always calls me, remembering David's birthday and day of passing. She visits the cemetery on these dates, and sometimes the children leave toys for David.

Throughout the years as I watch Michael, Nicole, and Brian grow up, I see David beside them. They are my measuring tape of his life as it would have been. Where would David be if he was still here? When they played together, they were like the four musketeers. Today they hang out with Amira. How happy David must be. Knowing that David is still participating in our lives has given me an unusual kind of fulfillment. When Michael and Nicole tell me they still feel David and talk to him, I am deeply touched. David is our guardian angel.

Seventeen years later my older cousin, Rosemary, with whom I am very close, had a grandson. This beautiful little boy, Kingston, was born on August 14, 2009, the anniversary date of David's passing. I now celebrate a new birth on this date.

Kingston's father's name is David. At one time as an adult, David lived with me. I experienced God's loving hand when I would come home and find David and Amira waiting for me. As I cooked dinner, I could hear them laughing, and when it was time to go to say good night, David would put his arms around me and give me a kiss on my cheek. Amira would follow with a kiss on my forehead. I would close my eyes in gratitude. My family. The way it was all playing out was and is amazing to me.

*Spirit asks: Are we all eternally connected, whether in body or in spirit?*

In front of the local church, David hiding behind a cross, Michael, Nicole, and Brian.

# CHAPTER 18

## A Matter of Time

*The veil that separates heaven and earth is thin. One day it will not exist.*
—Spirit

### Alexandra 1996

On this soulful, bright morning in the fourth year after David's passing, I saw him in my kitchen. How he has grown. And Amira is three years old. Both of my children are growing up.

I put Amira in her high chair and began to cook her oatmeal with bananas. I took her cereal bowl and poured in the warm cereal. As I turned to place the bowl in front of Amira, I froze. To my astonishment there was David sitting on a chair with his hands crossed on the table. His hair was lighter. He was taller. No longer a little boy. If I could put an age on him, I would say he looked around sixteen years old. He smiled and glowed in a soft golden light. He looked at me and then at Amira. We both smiled at him, and I could feel his thoughts.

He said, "Mom, I want you to know I am okay. I am happy to see you and Amira. Everything is going to be fine. Good things will happen soon that will make you happy. I will not be able to visit as often, but you will feel me. It takes a lot of energy to have you see me. I will be learning how to do this better, and when I have finished with my studies, I will visit you. I love you and Amira."

As he finished speaking, he disappeared, but his presence lingered like an aroma of sweet perfume. This happened in slow motion. When I looked at the clock behind Amira, only a few seconds had passed. Time was no longer measurable. I gave Amira her food, but she did not want to eat it. We were both filled with David's presence. I wondered how long before I would see my son again.

I had a dream that night. I was driving the silver Honda Accord involved in the actual accident. David was in the backseat. He looked like about three years old. I parked the car and opened the back door to get David out. I suddenly stepped on something that broke. I looked down and picked up a broken watch. Time had stopped. I looked at David and picked him up in my arms. I held him so tightly. I did not want to let him go ever again. Unexpectedly I heard a voice say, "It is only a matter of time." I woke up remembering that phrase.

***Spirit asks: What is time to the soul? Do we travel in dreamtime, present time, and future time all at the same ti***

# CHAPTER 19

## Creating Avalon

*Avalon, a place between heaven and earth.*
—Alexandra

### Alexandra, July 2001

My life as a healer continued, and it took many forms. I started a small business in the quaint town of Lafayette. I found a two-story cottage that had been converted into to a business building on Brown Avenue. I named it "Avalon, A Place for Body and Spirit." As clients walked up to the second floor from the parking lot, I arranged for a couple of guardian angel statues to greet them as they entered. I wanted my clients to feel they had entered into to a peaceful, sacred dwelling. They could hear soft flute and harp music playing with a resonating sound of Tibetan bowls. The scent of lavender permeated the entrance and guided them farther inside. Crystals balanced the chi in every room. Paintings by Waterhouse decorated the walls. His beautiful ladies of a magical Victorian time take one into different dimensions. Purple and gold curtains flowed like moving walls that allowed clients to slip in and out of the rooms.

I remember sitting in the middle of my yoga room, calling out to the universe to send me clients who needed my service. I visualized being in a lighthouse with a beam of light reaching out to my new community. In a couple of days a lovely woman named Clara stepped into my studio. She asked if I was available to give her a massage.

My healing room was ready. She filled out a client form, and I took her to my treatment room. When I walked in, she was lying on her back, and I could tell she had been crying. I asked her if she was okay, and she said she had been guided to me after her meditation this morning. It seemed she only lived a few block away. She had gone out for a walk and had been drawn to my place by the Arthurian design and gold/black colors on my sign. Walking up the stairs, she saw my brochure outside the door and read that I did massages. She was intrigued by the name of my business, and as she looked inside the window, she liked how spiritual it felt to her.

Then she said, "I am a medical psychologist, but I am also very spiritual. What I need is a shaman to do an egg cleansing on me. Do you do that?"

I was stunned. "Yes, I do. I am Mayan. It is in my lineage to heal this way."

Her look was that of astonishment, and then she said calmly, "That is why I am here. I need your help. My father is very ill. My brothers and sisters are arguing about putting him in a home-care facility. I know he does not want to leave his home. He has all his memories there, especially about my mother. I am the only one siding with him, and it has taken its toll. Can you help me?"

"Yes, I can," I said.

I excused myself and went to the kitchen, where I took out a chicken egg from the refrigerator. I poured water into a tall glass and brought it back to my healing room. I placed the egg in my right hand. The egg becomes a magnet, drawing out negative energies that should not be there. These energies come from negative thoughts or situations that remain stuck in a person.

I said a sacred prayer of protection and clearing. I began the cleansing by holding the egg about six inches away from the body. Quickly I started to feel the magnetic pull. I gently started a sweeping movement around the energy field of the body. As I passed the egg over the body, I could feel things being drawn out. Sometimes my hand would whirl and pull me in different directions. Then I felt I was transported into a bedroom. A beautiful glowing light emanated from the center of the room.

I heard a voice say, "He needs to stay in his home. It holds many special memories for him. If he is taken away, he will pass on quickly. Tell Clara she is right to protect her father. It is important he stays in his home. It is not time for him to leave yet."

I told Clara what I saw and heard. She seemed very relieved. I took the egg and cracked it into the glass of water. We waited a few minutes for the egg white to take shape. Within minutes it had taken the shape of a broken heart. I told her what we were looking at was the energy of her father's broken heart. This was what he had carried since his wife's passing. She acknowledged what we saw and said she would continue to be the spokesperson on her father's behalf. I finished my massage and healing treatment. We said good-bye, and she said she would be in touch with me for another treatment.

I received a call from Clara a few days afterward. She told me she had finally convinced her siblings to leave their father at home and hire a caregiver. Then a miracle happened. Her father had a dream about her mother. She told him that he was going to be fine, that he needed to take care of his health. She promised to wait for him in heaven. When he woke up, he remembered the dream in detail. He began to get dressed and could not find his shoes, so he got down on his hands and knees to look under the bed. He saw something glistening. He reached for it, and then he saw that it was his wife's wedding ring—the wedding ring she had been buried with. He got up, really excited, and called all his children. He shared what had happened and said he had been worried about her. He had wanted to go with her because he wanted to take care of her, but he knew now that she was fine. She had given him the perfect symbol as a message to help him understand that she was okay.

Clara was grateful that her father had gotten this message from her mother. It seems it had given him a new perspective on life and his willingness to heal himself. She was very grateful to me for helping her family find the best solution for her father. If he had been moved, he would not have experienced the miracle of finding the wedding ring.

Egg cleansings have led to many wondrous events. I always remain in awe of the healings that have taken place. A marvelous example is when Jan came to me because massages had helped her depression in the past. She was on medication, and she was about to quit her job. I began by giving her a healing massage followed by the egg cleansing. When I cracked the egg in the glass of water, what formed was a skull with two crossbones in detail. Immediately I recognized death. I asked her if she had been contemplating suicide. She said yes. She was unhappy with her life and did not like her supervisor at work. As soon as she said that, I saw her office with roses on her desk. I saw she was packing to leave for another office. I asked her if she could transfer to another position. She said she had not thought about it. I advised her when she returned to work to put roses on her desk as a reminder that God would help her transfer to a new job. I also asked her to smile at her supervisor and internally thank her for helping her move to a new position. Jan agreed to do this and said she would keep me informed if anything changed. After a few weeks it seems someone retired and a vacancy was posted for a new job. Jan applied for it, got it, and moved to a new office only a few minutes away from her home. It was a blessing. A door opened, giving her a new opportunity at a job that she enjoyed. Her sadness was gone.

Sometimes our blessing comes disguised as something else. This was the case with Sarah, a unique individual who held a high-powered job. She came to me for detoxification treatments. I used the aqua chi machine, a water-ionizing treatment that pulls out metal and toxic material. I prepared the treatment and put her feet in a warm footbath with the activated module. As she was seated and received the treatment, I could feel she needed to get something off her chest. I inquired, and she began to share her big problem. Sarah worked with a woman who was very flirtatious with the men in her office. At a recent dinner party she caught this woman flirting with her husband. Since then she always felt anger swelling whenever she was in close proximity to this woman. She kept referring to her as a snake and was troubled that she could lose control of her anger. I asked Sarah to think about what would make her happy in this situation. She thought about it and said she would be very happy if this woman moved to another office or got a new job.

We prayed on it, and I asked her if she would be open to doing an egg cleansing. After I explained to her what it was, she agreed. I prepared for it, and after I completed the treatment, I cracked the egg in a glass filled with water. Soon the egg white began to create a form. It became very clear that it looked like a snake with its mouth open. You could see the fangs as if it was ready to bite. We were left speechless. When we recovered, I advised her to take a salt bath before she went to sleep. Salt will remove any negative energy still looming. Sarah made another appointment for the following week, and we both went home.

When I got home, I could feel something was off. I told my husband, Richard, what had happened and said I believed something had attached itself to me. He volunteered to do an egg cleansing on me, his first time. When he cracked the egg in the glass filled with water, what we saw forming was the same snake. Somehow the energy that had been pulled out of Sarah had come home with me, which is very unusual. This snake energy wanted a new home or host. Being very careful, I needed to make sure this energy was completely removed. This time I took some sage and did a clearing in my home and everyone in it. It worked.

The following week when Sarah came to see me I told her what had happened. She was shocked, but what was more distressing was that her manager had informed her that she was being transferred to a new office. She was very upset that she would be moving to a different location with new clients and that they were giving her the responsibility of being completely in charge of the office. She was bewildered that she had not been asked but was told instead this would take place next week. As she continued to share her story, I started to smile. I asked her if the woman she disliked would be going with her.

She said, "No."

I said, "God has answered your prayer. You will no longer be working with her. She is gone out of your life. Not as you intended but in God's way, the best way." She sat there, dumbfounded. She started to laugh and said, "I need to call my husband and tell him the good news."

**Spirit asks:** *Do you believe that ancient methods of healing are timeless tools that always work, and anyone can do them? If you believe and trust, can you be a channel, with God as the source?*

# CHAPTER 20

## Henry's Choice

*It does not matter how you leave.
What matters is how you have loved.*
—Spirit

### Alexandra 2002

Henry was a gentle, bright teenager of fifteen years who heard voices. One day the tormenting voices would not stop. So he stopped them.

It was 7:30 on a cold evening, on March 24, eight years after David made his transition. I heard the phone ring, and a familiar voice said my name in a painful, somber tone. It was Albert, a friend for more than twenty-five years. What I heard that evening alarmed me. He held his words like a dam ready to burst. "Albert," I said, "what's wrong?"

"Henry is dead. He killed himself." Then his pain burst into relentless sobbing. I automatically reacted to embrace his pain with the memory of mine.

Eight years before I had made a similar phone call to Albert. Now I swirled in a time lapse, recalling so much. Our union as family started when Albert and Betty asked me to be godmother to their firstborn, Frances, a beautiful baby girl with shiny black hair and brown sparkly eyes. When David was born, I asked them to be his godparents, and they accepted. Henry was their second child. He and I had an unspoken agreement that I was his godmother as well. It seemed we had a spiritual contract with each other because when my daughter Amira was born, I asked Betty and Albert to be her godparents, which they accepted. To this day Frances and Amira see each other as sisters. I know that both our boys are in heaven as brothers.

After the phone call, quietness settled within me. I went to my bedroom. I lit a candle on my altar where I have pictures of David and the rest of my family in heaven. I looked for a picture of Henry and found one in my picture box, one in which he was much younger. I placed it on my altar and began to talk to Henry, God, and David.

Grief has so many different forms. This time I did not yell or scream. I sat down on my bed, closed my eyes, and kept visualizing Henry moving into the light and finding his way to God. I asked David to help him, and I started to see the two boys together surrounded in a radiant light, their friendship very much alive. My heart was inundated with irresistible devotion as I felt the love between them.

It was around one in the morning when I felt someone sitting on my side of the bed. I knew it was Henry.

"Baby boy, why did you do that?" I asked.

Henry answered in a slow, easy voice, "I couldn't stand the voices. I wanted to get them out of my head. They keep telling me things I don't want to hear, so I tried stopping them without thinking I could not come back."

"Henry," I said, "I can feel you are sad. I know you did not mean to do this. Do you want me to tell your mom and dad what you have just told me?"

"Yes, but I want to go back to my home and be with them."

"Your home is now with God, Henry. David will help you get there."

"I know. I am so sorry this happened." As he said this, I could feel his presence lifting from the bed.

"Henry, we all love you. You have left your body, but you are still alive. Go and heal with God. We will all be together soon. I promise you! It is only a matter of time. David will help you." His beautiful, gentle spirit left. I stayed awake, thinking of the past and the pain my dear friends were going through.

The following morning I left to be with Henry's family. As I drove on the old familiar highway, I looked at the trees, farmhouses, horses, and cows. *How can it all be the same and yet so different?* The road of destiny had taken a turn, and we the living cannot follow Henry's destiny. Memories of times together collide with this moment of torturous grief. It makes me aware that we are here for such a short time. I wonder how many summers we possibly have left together.

I am comforted that God has given David new goals and this new life is fulfilling him. I know David is happy. I believe this is true for Henry as well.

Taking your life does not lock you out of heaven because love never does that. We are love. God is love, and heaven is love.

**Spirit asks: Can love release all judgment? If so, how? Can we send energy that heals and guides those we love through prayer, no matter what the circumstances?**

# CHAPTER 21

## Writing, a Christmas Gift

### Alexandra

Christmas 2010, eighteen years later after David's passing, my aunt Orbelina was ninety-seven years old. This brought our family together at her home. We always celebrated Christmas with our traditional Salvadorean food, especially *pupusas* (white corn tortillas with melted cheese), plantains, and our grandmother's favorite, quesadilla (cheese coffee cake). We never missed the chance to drink *horchata*, a milky drink made out of native nuts and spices.

The big question that year was this: *What gifts do I give my family for Christmas when my funds are so limited and they have everything they need?* I turned to God, the source of all knowledge, and said, "God, reveal to me, give me a sign, fill my heart with your answer to do something special for my family."

Throughout the day I started to remember family stories that

I had heard as I was growing up. There was one in particular that I never got tired of hearing. I called it the firefly story. To this day when I hear my mother tell it, she becomes that little girl sharing her experience with her father, my grandfather, Papa Chepe.

By the end of the day I heard God say, "Write the firefly story and bake quesadillas. This is your Christmas gift to your family." I was greatly excited. I knew this was the perfect gift for my brother, sisters, cousins, aunts, and especially my mother. But me a writer? What would my family say? I had written many good and fun-filled speeches for toastmasters, but the thought of writing this story felt scary and thrilling at the same time. Then I heard David's voice say, "Mom, you know how to do this, and we will help you."

I pulled out my Apple laptop. As I stared into the blank screen, I said, "Okay, God, okay, David, let's do this together." A flood of words and images overtook me. I was enjoying so much pleasure. My experience was that of something coming alive from a movie screen. It was exhilarating that we could write something together. This was the beginning of finding my voice in union with God and David.

Christmas came with no trepidation. My gifts were bursting out of their bags and me. First we celebrated with the assortment of food, and then we handed out our gifts. I passed out my gift printed on light golden autumn-like paper, with round aromatic quesadillas wrapped in plastic wrap. I started to see some of my family members sit and read what I had given them. They would look up at me with love, softness, tenderness, and so much appreciation that I knew I had touched their souls. This is the story:

# Fireflies

El Salvador, the savior of Central America, birthing a small gentle, dark people. Ancient volcanic lands where the Mayans left their footprints and the conquistadores denied their existence by trying to erase them. Copal, the old shaman incense, stirs memories of jungles, erupting its legends. I can still feel the warning in the warm breezes that call "La Siguanava," the native goddess, stirring up the old fears before the Ten Commandments.

El Salvador sits as a tiny jewel, reflecting its brilliance only to the Pacific waters of our earth. Opulent minerals, sugar, and coffee plantations enticed the French court to live here. *The Little Prince* flew into the small town of Armenia one summer, establishing his creator Antoine de Saint Exupery and Consuelo Sunc'in in a stately manor. The Count and Countess de Saint Exupery made special invitations to balls providing delicate cuisine, splendid parades of French courtier, and French perfumes to help us breathe it all in.

I am told we have five reigning families. They made a pact that became law. No African slaves would be allowed in El Salvador. We had enough *mestisos*, those who are racially mixed, to keep us *pure* in different forms of slavery. Can it be that the shade of our skin, color, and shape of our eyes are still reasons why no one has given up the revolutions?

In the pueblo of Armenia lived a strong, tall, indigenous woman. Her hair was midnight, reflecting the moon, and her eyes captured you like a jaguar seeking its prey. Silveria was my great-grandmother. She healed with herbs, chants, medicine animals, and *limpiesas* (clearing of negative energy). Her hands were able to pull out toxic arrows filled with dark forces causing illness. People came searching for her, knowing they would be healed. Her payments were always elaborate—baskets filled with *platanos* (native bananas), *nances* (small sweet tropical fruit), mangos, chicken eggs for her cleansings, corn tamales, and *pupusas* (corn tortillas filled with cheese). She had great faith and trusted that when you did good, good came back. She had visions of her descendants. A son was born. No one remembers who the father was.

My grandfather, Don Jose Maria Zepeda, my Papa Chepe, was a

farmer of land and women. His pirate Spanish bloodline was strong, giving him blond hair and blue eyes. He was a natural psychic and medium, doing séances in his parlor while my grandmother, Trinidad, prayed with her rosary, calling the four directions of the cross.

The rooster's crow awakened the seventh day of July 1935. The youngest daughter of Don Jose and Dona Trinidad is celebrating her fifth birthday. The smell of corn tortillas and fried platanos wakes up the rest of the household. Preparation is an all-day event. The child has been waiting all year. She is an awakened one, a star child in the memory of Great-Grandmother Silveria. Her name is Rhinita, my mother.

The child runs through the corridors of the house, glowing with excitement as she dances with everything in sight. Don Jose is watching her with a cigar in his mouth. He admires his little one, thinks to himself, *She will save this family one day.* He has visions like his mother.

Tobacco, Don Jose's dog, gently guards the child around the house. Tobacco has many responsibilities, especially guarding Don Jose's secrets. Whenever Don Jose leaves home, a cigar goes in his pocket, with Tobacco at his side. Tobacco is tall and lean, the color of Don Jose's cigar, thus anointed with the name.

Visitors approach all day to pay their respects, bringing birthday gifts. Tobacco sniffs every gift. This is expected of him. He fulfills his duty. Rhinita smells each gift as well, mimicking Tobacco in agreement with a wink.

Toward the end of the day the workmen leave the field and approach the home of their patron to pay their respects. Holding their sombreros in their hands with their eyes lowered, they offer little gift of fruit or candy. Tobacco releases the child from his guard, where she quickly snatches the candy and runs away.

Only one of these workmen remains standing like shadow.

Anselmo is the oldest *campesino* who worked for Don Jose. God blessed him with all his senses except one. For some inexplicable reason God decided that his sight needed very little light. The blessing was that all the other senses remained awake while his eyes half-slept. Anselmo was shy around the star child. Her questions had the tendency to startle his near darkness. His replies jumped to explanations, spinning new fairy tales that must be told. Time was approaching. He was savoring the moment to give his birthday gift. He was starting to feel the weight of the day, so he sat on an old tree stump.

The child saw him and came to sit of like a ray of light beside him. He heard the crackling of paper, and she asked, "Indio Anselmo, would you like a piece of my chocolate?"

"Nina Rhinita," he replied, "I don't know what that is."

She giggled and said, "Open your mouth," and she slipped a dark piece into it.

"What do you think?" she asked.

Anselmo had never tasted anything like it. It took him a while to finish the rainbow of flavors illuminating his mouth. Slowly a tear escaped from his eyes.

"Why are you crying?" she asked.

"I have never tasted anything so delicious!"

She wiped his tear with her tiny finger and in a featherlike voice said, "I promise I will never forget you."

Anselmo smiled, acknowledging the vow, and said, "Now I can give you my gift." He reached into his pocket and pulled out a long, thin, weathered matchbox and placed it in her hands.

Rhinita was puzzled. "Why do you give me matches?" she asked surprised.

He squinted his eyes, grinned and said, "Open the box slowly."

With both hands she pulled and pushed the worn out matchbox. Suddenly lights emerged, flying delicately around her. She did not recognize them as they decorated her. She stood frozen, captured in a spell of light. It felt to her as if they were trying to pick her up and take her away, and it scared her.

"Papa, Papa!" she exclaimed, breaking the spell, and ran toward her father.

Don Jose jumped out of the hammock and looked at his child.

"Rhinita, they are fireflies. Don't be afraid," he reassured her. He was amazed as he looked at his daughter illuminated by the little flying lights.

Indio Anselmo approached, looked at both of them, and said joyfully, *"Feliz cumpleanos* (happy birthday), Nina Rhinita."

The years have passed, leaving a trail of lights catching up to my mother's memory of eighty-four years. She has kept her whispering promise to Indio Anselmo.

**Spirit asks: *When have words happened in your life?***

# CHAPTER 22

## I Am Alive

### David

It is 2011, and I am alive. "How can that be?" you might ask when my mother is writing this. I have surprised her by starting this chapter for her. I want her to know that all I do is filled with joy. I watch her as she grows and learns the beauty of life even in the most difficult of times. I see my sister, Amira, also growing up, going to college. I watch my whole family with the same tenderness that they feel for me. They have never forgotten me, and I am grateful. I have projects to complete, and we are working very hard to create peace in the world. Peace begins in the heart. Hold everything in your heart, all your emotions concerning all your experiences. Hold what you love and what gives you pain, because this will help transform pain into love. It is never the other way around.

You might want to know where I am. It is indescribable. Imagine when you are in love and everything is perfect. You are feeling the excitement of being alive and seeing those that you share love with. Our visions create our existence. For example, with a particular group we decide to imagine a lush forest that has an inviting, vibrant waterfall. We all think about this. We create it, and then we all enjoy the experience. It is continuously so. We have places of knowledge where we share our experience of the many lives we have lived. We learn from each other.

We do not sleep or eat because our nourishment surrounds us. We can relax and become dormant for a while, but it is only a matter of choice. The vibration of soul is what gives you the capacity of experiencing life here. If you continuously gravitate toward the love vibration, that is what you will experience here, and it gets stronger and stronger. It becomes a powerful, balanced magnet. We want all of life to be the energy source of love. Compassion is a passageway to love.

Time no longer exists here. We experience every moment. That is all. Looking older does not define age. Our appearance is in alignment to the vibration of who we are becoming. We can be formless or choose the form that is familiar. Sometimes I choose the pattern of David, the child that most family and friends remember. A few times I have released the image of a young adult with the same characteristics as David. Either way it is who you feel I am that is important. You will recognize me by experiencing me.

Everyone and every creature that has ever lived on earth is here with me. Our lives here are a constant celebration. But not everyone believes they deserve to be here. We work with these beings to help them love themselves. Eventually it happens. Since we are not distracted by time, we accept that all changes are manifested as they should be.

We are always with you. Love never separates. We are constantly waiting to assist you, whether you ask for it or not. We are one consciousness with you. We wait patiently for you to remember this. We give you signs. They come in dreams, miracles, synchronicity, and moments of kindness. Sometimes you will see or feel us. Smile, for you are loved.

***Spirit asks: What signs have you received?***

# CHAPTER 23

## *Grief*

### Alexandra

Elizabeth Kubler-Ross identified the five stages of grief: (1) denial, (2) anger, (3) bargaining, (4) depression, and (5) acceptance.

These five stages of grief were not stepping stones that in the end relieved me of my pain. My experience has shown me that all five stages happen at once. Like David, I experienced no linear sequence of events. In my grief I wanted the truth revealed, but I entered into a world of chaos that made no sense, a personal journey encrypted in pain. I became committed to deciphering its meaning and to raising my awareness about who I was in the world. Had a divine plan begun to unfold?

David passed away in the emergency room of John Muir Hospital. Two years later a synchronistic, surreal moment occurred. I was asked to massage a group of nurses at a private home. Just before I arrived, David told me to go get yellow roses for them. The message was so strong I did not hesitate. After each massage every nurse got a yellow rose. As I was getting ready to leave, I could hear them talking about work and the stress level of being in John Muir's emergency room.

I felt a cognitive vibration in my brain. Roses, healing massage, ER nurses—all the pieces started coming together. I felt as if I was reciprocating a thank-you from David. These nurses had taken care of him. This is why he wanted me to give them the roses. Subsequently I approached them with some apprehension and explained the gift. They were taken aback. Gradually two nurses looked at each other and said they remembered David. They would never forget how he fought to stay alive and how they all had been emotionally affected when they could not save him. There followed a silence of deep and overwhelming grief from everyone in the room. These nurses live in the experience of life and death. Grief and destiny brought us together.

Who was to blame for David's death? Me? God? Someone else? The most haunting question I had was, "Why did this happen to me? What did I do to deserve this? Was I being punished?" The answer to these questions never satisfied me until I realized that I was not the victim. The spiritual answer was that my child was still alive, though not in the physical realm. Even with all the miracles I had experienced, this was not an easy place to get to. The waves of anger, acceptance, depression, and surrender kept gathering and releasing me. The momentum of this experience filled and drained me with another year of being without him, another miracle to feel and see him, and finally I am alone without him. I moved in and out of these thoughts. I was in a constant flux. After many months I came to realize that I was not able to stop the death of my son. Forgiving myself began my journey of peace and mindful, conscious living.

I became aware that deep sadness had taken over my life. This sadness started to measure what was important in my life. I asked who my friends really were, what family members I wanted to be close with, if I wanted to stay married and have another child, if I wanted a new place to live and work.

A very alarming question also came up for me: "Did I have what is called the touch of death because this tragedy had happened to me?" I experienced the possibility of this when a close friend of mine from work invited me to a barbecue at her home. As I came in and began greeting everyone, a fellow coworker with his wife beside him raised his hand and said, "Please stay away. Do not touch me." I was stunned. I regained my composure and moved on. They both stayed out of sight, quite frightened of me, and soon afterward left. I was mortified that someone would react to me that way. Later I remembered that he had recently married and his wife was expecting a child.

Yes, friendships changed because some people did not know how to reach out, or their fear became so strong that it overpowered them. Then surprisingly, neighbors became friends. New people started to show up with ways to help, and old friends gave what they could.

Change becomes endless, and that is why grief weaves itself in and out for me. I look for the change that will make my life normal again. Normal it will never be, but my survival depends on change. Change has its greatest healing power when my mind chooses life.

***Spirit asks: How has grief changed you?***

# CHAPTER 24

## The Final Transition

In 1858 Louisa May Alcott, the author of *Little Women* kept a journal on the death of her sister, Elizabeth. She wrote the following:

> A curious thing happened, and I will tell it here, for Dr. G said it was a fact. A few moments after the last breath came, as Mother and I sat silently watching the shadow fall on the dear little face, I saw a light mist rise from the body, and float up and vanish in the air. Mother's eyes followed mine, and when I said, "What did you see?" she described the same light mist. Dr. G. said, it was the life departing visibly.

A few months later, Louisa made the following journal entry:

I don't miss her as I expected to do, for she seems nearer and dearer that before; and I am glad to know she is safe from pain and age in some world where her innocent soul must be happy. Death never seemed terrible to me, and now is beautiful; so I cannot fear it, but find it friendly and wonderful.

# What is death?

Death is the completion of a term in harmonious union between body, soul, and spirit.

The body is a healing organism. It will do everything it can to keep you alive. The body has its own language. When you are in danger, it constantly communicates by giving mild apprehensive and painful signals that are meant to warn you to stop what you're doing. When it cannot keep you alive, it will start to shut down. When the body is in unexpected danger, survival is limited, and when the term is up, the body will release the soul.

In 2008 Mark Mannucci, film director and writer, made a movie for *National Geographic* called *Moment of Death*. The exploration of many forms of death are filmed and documented. One common experience that is shown is how quickly the body shuts down in a traumatic situation. Whether through drowning, fire, crash, heart attack, or other forms of what we consider a sudden and tragic death, the body knows what to do immediately. In other words, in these situations the agony of death is not experienced. The organs and systems of the of the body stop functioning to allow a quick transition.

Whether the transition is sudden or stems from an illness that takes its time, death is a mystery that we must learn to live with. There is a group of people who have experienced death but whose term was not up, so they came back. This is called a near-death experience, and it is not new. In ancient times it was recorded in sacred Vedic texts, Judaic-Rabbinic literature, and especially the Egyptian *Book of the Dead*. In Egypt hieroglyphics speak the message of the eternal soul to the world. Currently the Near-Death Experience Research Foundation has thousands of documented cases. Many books have been written on the subject. A common experience is that these people felt no pain when their souls left their bodies.

In 1994 a coworker of mine named Wendy was shot in the head while waiting for a bus on the streets of Oakland, California. After several months of recovery she came back to work. Wendy immediately called me to share her experience. Wendy told me when she was shot, she did not feel anything. She fell to the ground and looked at the young man who had shot her take off in a screeching car. When the bus arrived, the driver called 911. Then a little girl dressed in white came out of the bus. She was glowing in a beautiful, soft golden light. She looked down at Wendy and told her that everything was going to be all right. Wendy quickly left her body and floated in a place filled with light and love. Time stopped for her. Then she heard a voice tell her that it was time to go back. She started to see pictures of her family crying for her at the hospital. When she saw herself covered in bandages with tubes, she was suddenly sucked back into to her body, and all the pain crashed into her. Wendy wanted to make sure that I knew David had not felt any pain when he left his body at the time of the accident. She wanted to ease my mind and comfort me with her experience.

## What is soul?

The soul is a spark of energy that ignites the body with consciousness.

All energy has a source. The energy source of the soul has many names—heaven, nirvana, God, just to name a few. The source is where we came from and will return. No matter what you call it, this energy source has no beginning and no end. It simply exists.

Our consciousness proves there is a soul because it talks to us. When I am alone and look out into my world, a silent dialogue begins. The miracle of this conversation is that I receive completely new information because the source is communicating with me. This is why prayer and meditation are so important to experience every day. I choose a time when I will not be interrupted. There is no clock to disturb me. I sometimes light a candle and look into its flame to remove all thoughts, allowing the mind to rest. I half-close my eyes. letting the light rays of the flame reach out to me. My breath is soft and calm. I connect with the silence. My consciousness dives into a pool of waves filled with light. There I experience God, and we begin our conversation or meditation.

Several months ago I watched on my computer a Dr. Oz episode on the human heart and its disease. Dr. Oz held a human heart in his hand. He showed us the inside of heart and pointed to a specific spot and said, "This is where the spark of life ignites the heart."

In 1907 Dr. Duncan MacDougall asked a very important question. If the soul exists, surely it weighs something, doesn't it? Dr. MacDougall created a bed with weights and placed patients on it who were beginning the process of death. Each time the patient passed away, the weight of the body became lighter. In 1970 Dr. Elizabeth Kubler-Ross also created the same experiment with some of her patients. The scales again showed results of a weight loss. Dr. Kubler-Ross wrote a book titled *Life after Life* documenting her case studies. In 2003 a film titled *21 Grams* was made. This title is based on the specific amount of weight that Dr. MacDougall had discovered as the weight of the soul.

## What is spirit?

Spirit is a perpetually evolving force of limitless energy. Everything is infused with spirit. Every molecule is activated by spirit energy that vibrates at different levels. Therefore, we are all connected because spirit flows through everything on this planet, giving us life.

## How do we connect and stay connected to God?

Affirm that you are not alone. Surround yourself with people who love you. Remember the love you have felt in the past from anyone.

We learn to survive the different levels of pain and sadness. It is in the accepting that our grief will always be a part of us that we can integrate sacred words like the "Lord's Prayer," a positive affirmation that will comfort, a quotation that inspires, and images that give us peace.

At night before you go to sleep, look into a mirror and see yourself with kindness and love. Let your soul talk to you.

Ask God to reveal answers to you and expect the miracle.

Give gratitude in words and actions and receive it in the same way.

## Reincarnation?

In 2008 I was meditating on reincarnation in Mount Shasta, California, when I became inspired to ask the following questions: "Where did I come from? What was my beginning?" Spirit guided me into a curious journey. It first began by saying, "It is in the blood." I was taken through images of the beginning of time, the evolution of mankind, my ancestors, and then me. I saw my body become a hologram with a complete map of my blood veins. Traveling through my veins were blood cells holding all the hologram images of evolution as I had just seen.

I was stunned. I realized that every blood cell in my body carried my personal history of all lives lived through my bloodline. I have continued meditating on this theme of awareness and have remembered much of where I came from. Recently I came across a program called *Ghost in Your Genes* by NOVA. I was taken aback to witness research scientists proving that all of who we are and where we come from is in our blood. The voices of our ancestors speak through our blood, and it still affects us, continuing to our descendants.

**Spirit asks: What resources have you discovered that have given you answers and understanding?**

# CHAPTER 25

## *Healer, Heal Thyself*

> *We are all healers.*
> —Alexandra

Some of us heal by touch. Others heal with words, sound, movement, imagery, witnessing, or being. Imagine for a moment that a field of energy pulsing with life has found a vehicle in which to express itself. We are the vehicles, and this life force is all-powerful, all-knowing, and eternal.

Science has proven that a life force exists in all matter, animate or inanimate. All matter moves in a particular vibration that defines itself. When a human body is created, its particular vibration and genetic coding establish how it will appear in the world. Then what makes us conscious? The soul, the spark of God.

Soul remembers where it came from. Soul reminds us of our purpose. Soul knows that there is no separation. We are here to gain personal knowledge of what we cannot experience in heaven. This is the soul's evolution!

We have everything we need to create what we want. We

create by focusing, giving our attention, better yet infusing it with our life force. We take conscious action. This is one of the greatest gifts God has given us.

When we have interior conversations about why things happen and especially about synchronicity, the questions and answers get clear. As we ask focused questions, we get focused answers. We wait with our hearts, and souls open to whatever way God will deliver the message. The answer will come through meditation, dreams, a person, a sign of some kind. It will take many forms. God is creative, and he will deliver his message in a way that we will understand profoundly.

When we look at human anatomy, we must go beyond the physical. Every system and organ within our body has energy patterns. These patterns connect the emotions with the physical parts that are being affected. Included in these patterns are the meridians and chakras that are identified in Eastern medicine. They exist in the human body and on our earth.

What is unique in humans is our brain, especially the frontal lobe of the brain. This is the area that gets activated when we meditate, visualize, or use our imagination. It creates energy or waves of thought. It is the magnet for direct attraction of what we need and desire.

## How do we take care of the emotional and physical body when in grief?

The body needs to be taken care of even if we feel it is no longer important. If we are to survive this experience, we must reach out to the things we need to keep us alive. We do this in honor of those who have passed on. Our central nervous system is undergoing an enormous amount of stress. Thoughts of all that has happened and all that needs to be done cycle endlessly like beads on a handheld rosary. Sleep evades us. There is no place to really rest or go to.

The following information helped my body get strong again. What I have listed below became my medicine to restore my health. Of course, it is important to consult your own health practitioner or medical doctor, as each of us is unique in some of our needs.

## Vitamins

Vitamin B complex calms the central nervous system and helps with inflammation caused by stress.

**Calcium-Magnesium:** Alkaline minerals that relax and release stress. Improves nerve, muscle and bone functions.

## Aromatherapy

You can use the power of plants to heal your body and release emotions. If it smells good to you, use it. If not, let it go. One of my favorites is lavender, from the Latin word *lavare*, meaning to wash away. Lavender calms the mind, so it will help you sleep. I invite you to pour a few drops in your bath, spray it on your pillow, or use it in lotion form to smell it throughout the day. Vanilla also has calming qualities.

## Salt Baths

Epsom or dead sea salts will soothe your body from physical and emotional pain. Soaking in steamy hot water with these salts will relax the muscles and nerves, thereby releasing tension. Your brain will also feel the benefit of this therapy, and stressful thoughts will diminish.

## Massage Therapy

This stimulates circulation, activates the autoimmune system, and can realign the body. This therapy calms the body and mind to help you rest and sleep. It also releases stress, emotions, and tension.

## Reiki Treatment

This treatment is a Japanese method that uses energy to heal. A Reiki practitioner will release sacred energy to relieve the body of stress and other symptoms you might have. It can also balance your chakras or energy centers so you can regain your strength, and it gives emotional relief. It can continue to enhance the body's ability to heal itself from physical and emotional pain.

## Yoga

A Hindu practice and system of exercise, yoga will gently strengthen your body by stretching muscles and the spinal column. You are taught many forms of breathing to assist you in cleansing your body of emotional and physical toxins. It introduces a focused meditation on sections of your body. Yoga trains you to hear the language of your body so that you can understand its warnings. Emotional memory releases are experienced at times. The *asanas* or postures serve to calm or give you energy, bringing balance to your body type.

## Tai Chi and Qi Gong

These Chinese systems of exercise with balanced body movements help one to move energy and release healing into the body.

## Grief Therapist or Group

You are not alone on this journey, although it can feel that way. Sometimes we need to share our complex feelings and get some insights. Each county has a local crisis center for weekly meetings and a referral list of therapists. The people in these organizations really care.

## Nutrition

Food is our medicine. Eating live food, especially organic, is critical to our well-being. Listen to your body as to when to eat. It is a way of life, not a diet. Connect with a nutritionist who will help you decide what to eat for your body type. Ayurvedic medicine assists in determining your body type or *dosha*. You review your body's imbalances and use food to bring it back to balance. For example, if you tend to run hot with lots of scattered energy, it is recommended to eat cooling foods to reduce the heat. If you are lethargic and have cold hands and feet, you need the warming food that will energize you.

## Stress

The body gives us many warnings through physical discomfort, such as headaches, neck, shoulder, and back pain, digestive problems, etc. Often these symptoms are telling us to stop and take care of ourselves. If we are in an emergency, the body will release adrenaline to give us energy and cortisol to clear our minds so that we can focus and resolve your situation. This is the good news. When we are under stress continuously, the body's immune system will weaken, which eventually affects our health. It is important to check if your pH is balanced. Most drug stores carry a kit that will help you check if you are acidic or alkaline. If you are alkaline, there is nothing to worry about. If you are acidic, your immune system is probably weak. It is recommended to put a tablespoon of apple cider vinegar in hot water or a salad to bring you back to alkaline balance.

## What is spiritual training?

Every day God gives us challenges in preparation for the day when we will be called to service. Our experiences become the tools that mold and develop our virtues, beliefs, and insights. We are participating in the evolution of ourselves.

When a situation repeats, it is the opportunity to do it differently and better. How will we use our awareness to make a difference here and create an outcome that best serves us?

I had an upsetting situation that repeated itself quite often. Since David's accident I would drive slowly. Sure enough, I would hear someone behind me honk. Then the agitated driver would pass me by fast, yelling with an obscene gesture on his hand. My typical reaction was to get upset and yell back, "You idiot!"

I decided it was time to change this movie and have a different ending. I did something David and I would do to each other. I started throwing kisses as soon as the drivers honked or drove by me. When I saw the shocked look their faces, I started to smile and then laugh. It made me feel good.

One late afternoon I was driving to my neighborhood video store. The usual aggravated honking sound erupted, so I started throwing kisses. The car sped around me and disappeared. When I pulled into the parking lot and parked, I recognized the car that had honked at me. Soon a teenage boy bounced out of the car and walked over to me.

He had a big smile on his face and said, "Excuse me, ma'am. When my father passed you, what did you do?"

I said, "I threw him kisses."

He laughed and said, "Right on. Dad, you owe me ten bucks. I was right."

The father sheepishly looked at me, pulled out his wallet, and gave his son money.

Very rarely do I get honked at anymore. My driving has not changed, but my attitude has. My basket of kisses are waiting, sitting beside me when I drive.

Awareness is developed by having a relationship with God, source, spirit, soul, community, and ourselves. All such communication becomes stronger when you are continuously engaged with it. Having inner conversations with spiritual sources develops intuition. It also opens us to connect with spiritual mentors and guides. When we commune with self, we discover we are not alone and someone is listening.

When we are grieving, our spiritual connections are extremely important. I encourage you to read books like *Embraced by the Light* by Betty J. Eadie, *Life after Death* by Deepak Chopra, *Reunions* by Raymond Moody, *Crossing Over* by John Edwards, *The Celestine Prophecy* by James Redfield, *The Power of Intention* by Wayne Dyer, *Heal Your Body* by Louise Hay, A research lecture by Klaus and Gundi Heinemann, "Orbs and Subtle Energies," April 29, 2012, at GreatMysteries.org. See also programs with William Tiller PhD, professor emeritus at Stanford University and Dr. Norm Shealy as well as Micheal Ledwith, PhD, professor of systematic theology at Maynooth College, Ireland.

# Our Challenges: Why do they continue?

Challenges are a continuous part of our reality. They take many forms. I like to call them the many faces of God. If we could truly see God in situations and in people, how would we react? Our experiences would vary.

My personal experience is that now instead of being reactive, I take my time in listening to a known or new face of God. My interaction takes on a new form, with lessons becoming clearer, especially my part in them. I stop taking the challenging situation personally and engage in it as if I were student watching it. The mind and body take on a detached and much calmer response because they are observing. We are able to ask, "What am I responsible for? How can I have a different outcome, and what is my lesson here?"

# What can disconnect us from healing?

What I have stated in the beginning of this chapter will nourish and help stabilize your healing experience. As I have said before, when we grieve, our bodies and minds will do what they can to keep us alive. If we self-medicate with alcohol, drugs, and other forms of distractions, it will create blocks to disconnect us from the most critical times of self-preservation. Eliminating harmful distractions will increase the spiritual flow of healing energy.

*Spirit asks: Does your inner voice communicate with you, and evolve in awareness and power?*

# CHAPTER 26

## Connecting to the Other Side

How can we connect to our children or other loved ones who are on the other side?

Connecting to the other side is a skill to be practiced. I have developed and organized personal knowledge that can be used by anyone. Over time as I observed my clients use my techniques, very special healings took place. I have compiled a method with key components that enable us to take action in connecting with our children or loved ones.

This information came from natural experiences that became stronger with time. As a child I would see and hear my ancestors communicating with me. My grandmother always wanted to know what they said and would encourage me to continue to have these experiences. Many times when I am doing my healing work my ancestors will visit me and help with the healing sessions. Other times beautiful guides imbued in light will show up to assist or share messages for me and my clients.

I would like to include what David and those on the other side have said and shown me. When our loved ones leave their physical bodies and go into God's realm, they are given tasks, and new lives begin for them. Many quickly take on their new lives with excitement. There are those like David who ask to stay spiritually connected to help their families heal. David and other guides have said that each soul has a group of guardians that helps it understand where it is and its purpose while it is making its transition. Sometimes these guardians are people we have known on earth, or they are parts of our heavenly family. Our guardians help many accept that they have died and they are forgiven. They show them the way to a new life with God. The vibration of love and prayer helps release those who are unable to move on. Whatever the situation is, God is taking care of them.

Using my imagination I created a place called "my garden in heaven". It is a place I go to when I meditate. It has an assortment of beautiful trees, including cherry trees and weeping willows. Vibrant red roses, purple irises, pink tulips, and lavender fill the air with their aroma. There are little pathways ending in sitting areas where butterflies and hummingbirds dance. The sound of a waterfall fills the background, and you can walk to a nearby pond surrounded by water lilies and lotus blossoms. It is here I find David, my grandmother, my father, and loved ones when I need them. The one interesting thing about my garden in heaven is that a few years ago I was surprised to see people I had no relationship with. What I mean is I did not recognize everyone. Those I did I had not seen in many years. They would wave and smile at me. I believe I was shown a place that activated all my sense so that I could stay connected with my loved ones. This place always welcomes me. With time I realized I did not create this garden in heaven. It has always existed. I simply finally saw it.

This is the practice I have used to communicate with my ancestors, grandparents, father, angelic guides, and especially David.

## Spiritual Connectors

Connectors are pathways that open our awareness and accelerate our consciousness of God.

## Love Connector

Love is the most powerful force that exists, and it connects us to the other side immediately. Practice feeling love in your heart and immerse yourself in it. Then send it to your children or loved ones. Do this several times a day. Love expands, links, and transcends us into God's realm. See them enveloped in your love as memories rise and sustain this feeling for as long as you can. Let love heal all the emotions that will unfold. It will give relief to the excruciating pain of loss. Stay in your heart memory and connect with your love energy. If you feel it, they feel it too.

## Language Connector

Ask for a sign. God has given us the ability to ask for what we want—the power of the spoken word. Your awareness is then activated to look for signs, and they will be given to you. It could be that your child's favorite bird keeps appearing around your home or that someone gives you flowers that your grandmother used to like or that you turn on the radio and at that very moment hear a song your child used to sing. Become aware of relevant symbolism. It will connect you to things, places, and memories that mean something special to you. When these signs appear, acknowledge the communication they are connecting.

## Meditation Connector

Meditation is the mind connecting to God. I call it my divine appointment. Meditation also calms the central nervous system so you can experience peace throughout your body. Create a time when you can meditate in silence. This creates a space in which to hear the communication. Meditating in silence is simply finding a place where you will not be disturbed and can quiet the mind. Sit comfortably, close your eyes, and begin taking slow, deep breaths that will allow your body and mind to relax. Focus your mind on that place between the brows so no thoughts can come in. Be still and silent. Practice this every day for about twenty minutes. Eventually you will hear your inner voice or the voice of your child or loved one communicating with you.

## Dream Connector

Dreams are a doorway to a dimension that your child or loved one can connect to. If you are concerned about how you child or loved one is doing or you need advice from a loved one, ask for it. Before you go to sleep at night, set an intention. Repeat it over and over in your mind until you fall asleep. Your connection in dreamtime will sometimes take a few days.

For example, I remembered that David never got to see Disneyland and that I had promised to take him. I had been waiting for him to get a little older so he could enjoy more of the rides. When I would think of Disneyland, a deep sadness of regret would set in. Therefore, I created an intention to take him to Disneyland, and I also wanted to make sure he still wanted to do this. I began repeating, "David, let's go to Disneyland together if you still want to go." By the third evening it happened. There we were in Frontier Land, laughing and running around. I had a strong sensation of holding his hand. When I woke up, I could still feel his presence as if he was holding me. All my emotions came running out as I released them in gratitude for this blessed experience.

## Prayer Affirmation Connector

Prayer is an expression of faith. To pray is to believe that you can make a difference. It aligns you to God. Prayer in the form of affirmations creates a deep connection to God, for they are divinely inspired to personally help. Affirmations are a tool of manifestation. When we affirm, we create. My prayer affirmations are short and easy to remember throughout the day. It is important to write your affirmations down and repeat them often. This keeps it active with God's energy flowing through them. In other words it stays plugged into the source. Here are a few examples of prayer affirmations I use:

- I am one with God and my child (name) always.
- It is revealed to me how happy and safe my child (name) is.
- I hear and see all of God's messages concerning my child (name) in heaven.
- My love for you keeps me connected at all times. There is no separation.
- My heart is open to receive messages from my child or loved one (name).
- I can feel your loving presence.

## Rose Connector

Roses represent love, and they lift our spirits when we are sad and grieving. In aromatherapy they carry the highest vibration for healing. When we surround ourselves by their scent and presence, we connect to their healing power. As we deeply breathe in the therapeutic aroma of roses, we smile, and our bodies respond to its curative abilities. We absorb their beauty through our eyes, and we experience fulfillment, degrees of happiness, and hope. Roses carry the energy of love. That is why throughout human history we give roses as symbols of our love. They also transmit an aura of protection that is quickly felt. I find that I sleep better with a rose on my nightstand. As I close my eyes, it is the last thing I see beside the pictures of my children. I feel safe, and I send these and other thoughts of affection to them. I place roses around my home to reinforce my connection to all my loved ones, no matter where they are.

Surround yourself with roses and choose a color that attracts you the most. The color becomes a healing aspect that your body and soul need to restore you. As you connect to this energy, you become receptive to the miracle of love. What flows through you moves freely to your child or loved one, and then it comes back. A circuit of affection, caring, tenderness, and kindness is established. This connection is eternal because its source is God, and God is love.

As I was writing this chapter, I received an understanding as to one of its important purposes. A spiritual download, as I call them, clued me in that this is how my daughter, Amira, will connect with me when I have joined my family in heaven. As I realized this, I was overwhelmed and struck with powerful thoughts and emotions, giving me a deeper understanding as to why I wrote this book. The connection expands. This connection will continue forever. Time and the physical body are no longer the gatekeepers of this dimension. We have entered and connected to God's universe.

**Spirit asks: *How have you connected to the other side? If not, are you willing to try?***

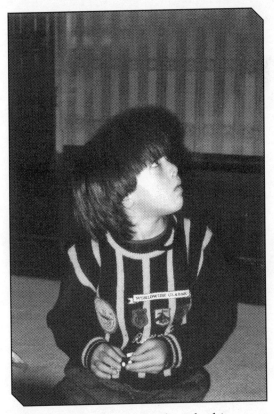

My favorite picture of David as he is looking up at me.

## Ode on Intimations of Immortality-continued

There was a time when meadow, grove, and stream,
The earth, and every common sight,
To me did seem
Apparell'd in celestial light,
The glory and freshens of a dream.
It is not now as it had been of yore,
Turn wheresoe'er I may,
By night or day,
The things which I have seen I can see no more.

What though the radiance which was once so bright
be now forever taken from my sight,
Though nothing can bring back the hour
Of splendour in the grass, of glory in the flower,
We will grieve not, rather find
Strength in what remains behind,
In the primal sympathy
Which having been must ever be,
In the soothing thoughts that spring
Out of human suffering,
In the faith that looks though death,
In years that bring the philosophic mind.
Thoughts that do often lie too deep for tears.

The innocent brightness of a new-born day
Is lovely yet;
Thanks to the human heart by which we live,
Thanks to it's tenderness, its joys, and fears.

—William Wordsworth

# Conclusion
# The Oak Tree Speaks

Wet, swishing, swirling sounds wake me from a dream. As usual I face the highway. A green sleek vehicle parks in front of me. A graceful woman with golden hair gets out and walks toward me. She looks familiar, but I do not recognize her until she puts her arms around me and I experience her tender heart beating with mine. Her brave voice shares what happened to her child after that painful day. Her tears are different. They express calm acceptance, comfort, and hope. I no longer see shadows, only a silhouette filled with light. She slowly releases her embrace, and traces of her love keep us connected. I know I will never see her again. It does not matter. We are linked in moments that escape time.

As she disappears, I observe the drizzle captured by my few remaining crimson leaves. They can no longer keep me warm. Peering into each mesmerizing droplet, I find reflections of earth, heaven, and its stars. For decades I have witnessed people experiencing moments of vast personal importance. These moments held me captive. As I shed this mantle of moments, I witness myself resonating with the desire to be.

A glimmer, a glow, a beam illuminates the way, and I choose to follow the dream. I become aware this voyage takes me into splendor to meet life in its transcendent majesty.

*Spirit says: As you drive past, notice those makeshift roadside memorials, the handmade crosses and flowers for those who departed suddenly, and are remembered in love. Someday someone will remember you. Let it also be for love. Live, Share, Give, Rejoice, now!*

# About the Author

Alexandra De Avalon is a spiritual teacher, artist, and shaman master healer in Pleasant Hill, California. She has been mentored by great spiritual teachers who have guided her to inspire and mentor others. As a watercolorist, she engages with energy that wants to manifest itself on canvas. This has become a healing art for her.

Alexandra works with clients on a deep spiritual level. She is a shaman master healer, and her Mayan ancestral roots have enhanced her physical and emotional healing abilities, which led her to discover new methods of healing. She shares her wisdom to assist others in their self-discovery and to connect with the healer and teacher within.

Alexandra's extraordinary experience with David has been documented in the *Contra Costa Times* of Northern California. Alexandra appeared on *The Other Side*, a television program filmed at Hollywood Studios in Burbank, California. She was also a frequent guest on the *Neighborhood Television Program* of Walnut Creek. Her interviews have always given comfort to viewers, making her a sought-after speaker.

Alexandra can be contacted at:

Email address: alexandradeavalon@me.com
www.facebook.com/alexandra.deavalon
www.linkedin.com